PEARSON

ALWAYS LEARNING

Leadership and Professionalism
Volume 1

Second Custom Edition for
The University of Iowa Career Leadership Academy

Taken from:

Professionalism: Skills for Workplace Success, Third Edition
by Lydia E. Anderson and Sandra B. Bolt

*Everything You Need to Know at Work: A Complete
Manual of Workplace Skills*
by Ciara Woods

Cover photograph courtesy of Tim Schoon/University of Iowa.

Taken from:

Professionalism: Skills for Workplace Success, Third Edition
by Lydia E. Anderson and Sandra B. Bolt
Copyright © 2011, 2008 by Pearson Education, Inc.
Published by Prentice Hall
Upper Saddle River, New Jersey 07458

Everything You Need to Know at Work: A Complete Manual of Workplace Skills
by Ciara Woods
Copyright © 2002 by Pearson Education, Inc.
Published by Prentice Hall Business
Harlow, Great Britain

Pearson Learning Solutions, 501 Boylston Street, Suite 900, Boston, MA 02116
A Pearson Education Company
www.pearsoned.com

Printed in the United States of America

1 2 3 4 5 6 7 8 9 10 V0ZN 17 16 15 14 13 12

000200010271626924

EB/OP

ISBN 10: 1-256-82471-2
ISBN 13: 978-1-256-82471-8

Copyright Acknowledgments

Chapter 1

"Introduction to Leadership," by Peter G. Northouse, reprinted from *Leadership: Theory and Practice*, Sixth Edition (2013), Sage Publications, Inc.

Chapter 2

"Chapter 3: The Relational Leadership Model," by Susan R. Komives, Nance Lucas, and Timothy Mahon, reprinted from *Exploring Leadership: For College Students Who Want to Make a Difference*, Second Edition (2007), by permission of John Wiley & Sons, Inc.

"Relational Leadership Is About Process," by Susan R. Komives, Nance Lucas, and Timothy Mahon, reprinted from *Exploring Leadership: For College Students Who Want to Make a Difference*, Second Edition (2007), by permission of John Wiley & Sons, Inc.

Chapter 5

"Stages of Group Development" and "Examples of Common Roles in Groups," by Susan R. Komives, Nance Lucas, and Timothy Mahon, reprinted from *Exploring Leadership: For College Students Who Want to Make a Difference*, Second Edition (2007), by permission of John Wiley & Sons, Inc.

Chapter 6

"Understanding Others," by Susan R. Komives, Nance Lucas, and Timothy Mahon, reprinted from *Exploring Leadership: For College Students Who Want to Make a Difference*, Second Edition (2007), by permission of John Wiley & Sons, Inc.

Chapter 7

"Why we hate PowerPoints and how to fix them," by Nancy Duarte, reprinted from *CNN.com* (2008), by permission of CNN.

Chapter 10

"What's My Communication Style?," by E. M. Russo, reprinted from *What's My Communication Style*, Second Edition (2011), by permission of HRDQ.

"Ten ways that 'good' communication styles vary across cultures," reprinted from *Multicultural Customer Service: Providing Outstanding Service Across Cultures*, edited by L. Aguillar and L. Stokes (1996), by permission of McGraw-Hill Companies.

Chapter 12

"Six strategies for dealing with difficult people," by Diane Berenbaum (2007), reprinted by permission of the author.

Appendix

"Summary of Leadership Theories/Approaches," by Susan R. Komives, Nance Lucas, and Timothy Mahon, reprinted from *Exploring Leadership: For College Students Who Want to Make a Difference*, Second Edition (2007), by permission of John Wiley & Sons, Inc.

Contents

Phase II   The Leader Who Understands Others

Chapters 3, 4, 5, 8, and 9 are taken from *Professionalism:
Skills for Workplace Success,* Third Edition,
by Lydia E. Anderson and Sandra B. Bolt.

Chapters 6 and 11 are taken from *Everything You Need to Know
at Work: A Complete Manual of Workplace Skills,*
by Ciara Woods.

Phase I: The Self-Aware Leader

Introduction to Leadership

by Peter G. Northouse

Courtesy of Shutterstock.

Leadership is a highly sought-after and highly valued commodity. In the 15 years since the first edition of this book was published, the public has become increasingly captivated by the idea of leadership. People continue to ask themselves and others what makes good leaders. As individuals, they seek more information on how to become effective leaders. As a result, bookstore shelves are filled with popular books about leaders and advice on how to be a leader. Many people believe that leadership is a way to improve their personal, social, and professional lives. Corporations seek those with leadership ability because they believe they bring special assets to their organizations and, ultimately, improve the bottom line. Academic institutions throughout the country have responded by providing programs in leadership studies.

In addition, leadership has gained the attention of researchers worldwide. A review of the scholarly studies on leadership shows that there is a wide variety of different theoretical approaches to explain the complexities of the leadership process (e.g., Bass, 1990; Bryman, 1992; Bryman, Collinson, Grint, Jackson & Uhl-Bien, 2011; Day & Antonakis, 2012; Gardner, 1990; Hickman, 2009; Mumford, 2006; Rost, 1991). Some researchers conceptualize leadership as a trait or as a behavior, whereas others view leadership from an information-processing perspective or relational standpoint. Leadership has been studied using both qualitative and quantitative methods in many contexts, including small groups, therapeutic groups, and large organizations. Collectively, the research findings on leadership from all of these areas provide a picture of a process that is far more sophisticated and complex than the often-simplistic view presented in some of the popular books on leadership.

This book treats leadership as a complex process having multiple dimensions. Based on the research literature, this text provides an in-depth description and application of many different approaches to leadership. Our emphasis is on how theory can inform the practice of leadership. In this book, we describe each theory and then explain how the theory can be used in real situations.

Leadership Defined

There are many ways to finish the sentence, "Leadership is . . ." In fact, as Stogdill (1974, p: 7) pointed out in a review of leadership research, there are almost as many different definitions of *leadership* as there are people who have tried to define it. It is much like the words *democracy, love,* and *peace.* Although each of us intuitively knows what we mean by such words, the words can have different meanings for different people. As Box 1-1 shows, scholars and practitioners have attempted to define leadership for more than a century without universal consensus.

Ways of Conceptualizing Leadership

In the past 60 years, as many as 65 different classification systems have been developed to define the dimensions of leadership (Fleishman et al., 1991). One such classification system, directly related to our discussion, is the scheme proposed by Bass (1990, pp. 11–20). He suggested that some definitions view leadership as the *focus of group processes.* From this perspective, the leader is at the

Box 1-1   The Evolution of Leadership Definitions

While many have a gut-level grasp of what leadership is, putting a definition to the term has proved to be a challenging endeavor for scholars and practitioners alike. More than a century has lapsed since leadership became a topic of academic introspection, and definitions have evolved continuously during that period. These definitions have been influenced by many factors from world affairs and politics to the perspectives of the discipline in which the topic is being studied. In a seminal work, Rost (1991) analyzed materials written from 1900 to 1990, finding more than 200 different definitions for leadership. His analysis provides a succinct history of how leadership has been defined through the last century:

1900–1929

Definitions of leadership appearing in the first three decades of the 20th century emphasized control and centralization of power with a common theme of domination. For example, at a conference on leadership in 1927, leadership was defined as "the ability to impress the will of the leader on those led and induce obedience, respect, loyalty, and cooperation" (Moore, 1927, p. 124).

1930s

Traits became the focus of defining leadership, with an emerging view of leadership as influence rather than domination. Leadership is also identified as the interaction of an individual's specific personality traits with those of a group, noting that while the attitudes and activities of the many are changed by the one, the many may also influence a leader.

1940s

The group approach came into the forefront with leadership being defined as the behavior of an individual while involved in directing group activities (Hemphill, 1949). At the same time, leadership by persuasion is distinguished from "drivership" or leadership by coercion (Copeland, 1942).

1950s

Three themes dominated leadership definitions during this decade:

- **continuance of group theory,** which framed leadership as what leaders do in groups;
- **leadership as a relationship that develops shared goals,** which defined leadership based on behavior of the leader; and
- **effectiveness,** in which leadership is defined by the ability to influence overall group effectiveness.

1960s

Although a tumultuous time for world affairs, the 1960s saw harmony amongst leadership scholars. The prevailing definition of leadership as *behavior* that influences people toward shared goals was underscored by Seeman (1960) who described leadership as "acts by persons which influence other persons in a shared direction" (p. 53).

(continued)

Box 1-1   The Evolution of Leadership Definitions (*continued*)

1970s

The group focus gave way to the organizational behavior approach, where leadership became viewed as "initiating and maintaining groups or organizations to accomplish group or organizational goals" (Rost, 1991, p. 59). Burns's (1978) definition, however, is the most important concept of leadership to emerge: "Leadership is the reciprocal process of mobilizing by persons with certain motives and values, various economic, political, and other resources, in a context of competition and conflict, in order to realize goals independently or mutually held by both leaders and followers" (p. 425).

1980s

This decade exploded with scholarly and popular works on the nature of leadership, bringing the topic to the apex of the academic and public consciousnesses. As a result, the number of definitions for leadership became a prolific stew with several persevering themes:

- **Do as the leader wishes.** Leadership definitions still predominantly deliver the message that leadership is getting followers to do what the leader wants done.

- **Influence.** Probably the most often used word in leadership definitions of the 1980s, *influence* is examined from every angle. In an effort to distinguish leadership from management, however, scholars insist that leadership is *noncoercive* influence.

- **Traits.** Spurred by the national bestseller *In Search of Excellence* (Peters & Waterman, 1982), the leadership-as-excellence movement brought leader traits back to the spotlight. As a result, many people's understanding of leadership is based on a trait orientation.

- **Transformation.** Burns (1978) is credited for initiating a movement defining leadership as a transformational process, stating that leadership occurs "when one or more persons engage with others in such a way that leaders and followers raise one another to higher levels of motivation and morality" (p. 83).

Into the 21st Century

After decades of dissonance, leadership scholars agree on one thing: They can't come up with a common definition for leadership. Debate continues as to whether leadership and management are separate processes, while others emphasize the trait, skill, or relational aspects of leadership. Because of such factors as growing global influences and generational differences, leadership will continue to have different meanings for different people. The bottom line is that leadership is a complex concept for which a determined definition may long be in flux.

SOURCE: Adapted from *Leadership for the Twenty-First Century*, by J. C. Rost, 1991, New York: Praeger.

See also Appendix: Summary of Leadership Theories/Approaches.

center of group change and activity and embodies the will of the group. Another set of definitions conceptualizes leadership from a *personality perspective*, which suggests that leadership is a combination of special traits or characteristics that some individuals possess. These traits enable those individuals to induce others to accomplish tasks. Other approaches to leadership define it as an *act* or a *behavior*—the things leaders do to bring about change in a group.

In addition, some define leadership in terms of the *power relationship* that exists between leaders and followers. From this viewpoint, leaders have power that they wield to effect change in others. Others view leadership as a *transformational process* that moves followers to accomplish more than is usually expected of them. Finally, some scholars address leadership from a *skills perspective*. This viewpoint stresses the capabilities (knowledge and skills) that make effective leadership possible.

Definition and Components

Despite the multitude of ways in which leadership has been conceptualized, the following components can be identified as central to the phenomenon: (a) Leadership is a process, (b) leadership involves influence, (c) leadership occurs in groups, and (d) leadership involves common goals. Based on these components, the following definition of leadership is used in this text:

> *Leadership* is a process whereby an individual influences a group of individuals to achieve a common goal.

Defining leadership as a *process* means that it is not a trait or characteristic that resides in the leader, but rather a transactional event that occurs between the leader and the followers. *Process* implies that a leader affects and is affected by followers. It emphasizes that leadership is not a linear, one-way event, but rather an interactive event. When leadership is defined in this manner, it becomes available to everyone. It is not restricted to the formally designated leader in a group.

Leadership involves *influence*. It is concerned with how the leader affects followers. Influence is the sine qua non of leadership. Without influence, leadership does not exist.

Leadership occurs in *groups*. Groups are the context in which leadership takes place. Leadership involves influencing a group of individuals who have a common purpose. This can be a small task group, a community group, or a large group encompassing an entire organization. Leadership is about one individual influencing a group of others to accomplish common goals. Others (a group) are required for leadership to occur. Leadership training programs that teach people to lead themselves are not considered a part of leadership within the definition that is set forth in this discussion.

Leadership includes attention to *common goals*. Leaders direct their energies toward individuals who are trying to achieve something together. By *common*, we mean that the leaders and followers have a mutual purpose. Attention to common goals gives leadership an ethical overtone because it stresses the need for leaders to work with followers to achieve selected goals. Stressing mutuality lessens the possibility that leaders might act toward followers in ways that are forced or unethical. It also increases the possibility that leaders and followers will work together toward a common good (Rost, 1991).

Throughout this text, the people who engage in leadership will be called *leaders*, and those toward whom leadership is directed will be called *followers*. Both leaders and followers are involved together in the leadership process. Leaders need followers, and followers need leaders (Burns, 1978; Heller & Van Til, 1983; Hollander, 1992; Jago, 1982). Although leaders and followers are closely linked, it is the leader who often initiates the relationship, creates the communication linkages, and carries the burden for maintaining the relationship.

In our discussion of leaders and followers, attention will be directed toward follower issues as well as leader issues. Leaders have an ethical responsibility to attend to the needs and concerns of followers. As Burns (1978) pointed out, discussions of leadership sometimes are viewed as elitist because of the implied power and importance often ascribed to leaders in the leader-follower relationship. Leaders are not above or better than followers. Leaders and followers must be understood in relation to each other (Hollander, 1992) and collectively (Burns, 1978). They are in the leadership relationship together—and are two sides of the same coin (Rost, 1991).

Leadership Described

In addition to definitional issues, it is also important to discuss several other questions pertaining to the nature of leadership. In the following section, we will address questions such as how leadership as a trait differs from leadership as a process; how appointed leadership differs from emergent leadership; and how the concepts of power, coercion, and management differ from leadership.

Trait Versus Process Leadership

We have all heard statements such as "He is born to be a leader" or "She is a natural leader." These statements are commonly expressed by people who take a trait perspective toward leadership. The trait perspective suggests that certain individuals have special innate or inborn characteristics or qualities that make them leaders, and that it is these qualities that differentiate them from nonleaders. Some of the personal qualities used to identify leaders include unique physical factors (e.g., height), personality features (e.g., extraversion), and other characteristics (e.g., intelligence and fluency; Bryman, 1992).

To describe leadership as a trait is quite different from describing it as a process (Figure 1-1). The trait viewpoint conceptualizes leadership as a property or set of properties possessed in varying degrees by different people (Jago, 1982). This suggests that it resides *in* select people and restricts leadership to those who are believed to have special, usually inborn, talents.

The process viewpoint suggests that leadership is a phenomenon that resides in the context of the interactions between leaders and followers and makes leadership available to everyone. As a process, leadership can be observed in leader behaviors (Jago, 1982), and can be learned. The process definition of leadership is consistent with the definition of leadership that we have set forth in this chapter.

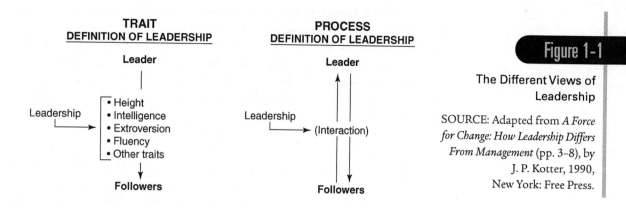

Figure 1-1

The Different Views of Leadership

SOURCE: Adapted from *A Force for Change: How Leadership Differs From Management* (pp. 3–8), by J. P. Kotter, 1990, New York: Free Press.

Assigned Versus Emergent Leadership

Some people are leaders because of their formal position in an organization, whereas others are leaders because of the way other group members respond to them. These two common forms of leadership are called *assigned leadership* and *emergent leadership.* Leadership that is based on occupying a position in an organization is assigned leadership. Team leaders, plant managers, department heads, directors, and administrators are all examples of assigned leadership.

Yet the person assigned to a leadership position does not always become the real leader in a particular setting. When others perceive an individual as the most influential member of a group or an organization, regardless of the individual's title, the person is exhibiting emergent leadership. The individual acquires emergent leadership through other people in the organization who support and accept that individual's behavior. This type of leadership is not assigned by position; rather, it emerges over a period through communication. Some of the positive communication behaviors that account for successful leader emergence include *being verbally involved, being informed, seeking others' opinions, initiating new ideas,* and *being firm but not rigid* (Fisher, 1974).

In addition to communication behaviors, researchers have found that personality plays a role in leadership emergence. For example, Smith and Foti (1998) found that certain personality traits were related to leadership emergence in a sample of 160 male college students. The individuals who were more dominant, more intelligent, and more confident about their own performance (general self-efficacy) were more likely to be identified as leaders by other members of their task group. Although it is uncertain whether these findings apply to women as well, Smith and Foti suggested that these three traits could be used to identify individuals perceived to be emergent leaders.

Leadership emergence may also be affected by gender-biased perceptions. In a study of 40 mixed-sex college groups, Watson and Hoffman (2004) found that women who were urged to persuade their task groups to adopt high-quality decisions succeeded with the same frequency as men with identical instructions. Although women were equally influential leaders in their groups, they were rated significantly lower than comparable men were on leadership. Furthermore, these influential women were also rated as significantly less likable than comparably influential men were. These results suggest that there continue to be barriers to women's emergence as leaders in some settings.

A unique perspective on leadership emergence is provided by social identity theory (Hogg, 2001). From this perspective, leadership emergence is the degree to which a person fits with the identity of the group as a whole. As groups develop over time, a group prototype also develops. Individuals emerge as leaders in the group when they become most like the group prototype. Being similar to the prototype makes leaders attractive to the group and gives them influence with the group.

The leadership approaches we discuss in the subsequent chapters of this book apply equally to assigned leadership and emergent leadership. When a person is engaged in leadership, that person is a leader, whether leadership was assigned or emerged. This book focuses on the leadership process that occurs when any individual is engaged in influencing other group members in their efforts to reach a common goal.

Leadership and Power

The concept of power is related to leadership because it is part of the influence process. Power is the capacity or potential to influence. People have power when they have the ability to affect others' beliefs, attitudes, and courses of action. Ministers, doctors, coaches, and teachers are all examples of people who have the potential to influence us. When they do, they are using their power, the resource they draw on to effect change in us.

The most widely cited research on power is French and Raven's (1959) work on the bases of social power. In their work, they conceptualized power from the framework of a dyadic relationship that included both the person influencing and the person being influenced. French and Raven identified five common and important bases of power: referent, expert, legitimate, reward, and coercive (Table 1-1). Each of these bases of power increases a leader's capacity to influence the attitudes, values, or behaviors of others.

Table 1-1   Five Bases of Power

Referent Power	Based on followers' identification and liking for the leader. A teacher who is adored by students has referent power.
Expert Power	Based on followers' perceptions of the leader's competence. A tour guide who is knowledgeable about a foreign country has expert power.
Legitimate Power	Associated with having status or formal job authority. A judge who administers sentences in the courtroom exhibits legitimate power.
Reward Power	Derived from having the capacity to provide rewards to others. A supervisor who gives rewards to employees who work hard is using reward power.
Coercive Power	Derived from having the capacity to penalize or punish others. A coach who sits players on the bench for being late to practice is using coercive power.

SOURCE: Adapted from "The Bases of Social Power," by J. R. French Jr. and B. Raven, 1962, in D. Cartwright (Ed.), *Group Dynamics: Research and Theory* (pp. 259–269), New York: Harper & Row.

Table 1-2	Types and Bases of Power
Position Power	**Personal Power**
Legitimate	Referent
Reward	Expert
Coercive	

SOURCE: Adapted from *A Force for Change: How Leadership Differs From Management* (pp. 3–8), by J. P. Kotter, 1990, New York: Free Press.

In organizations, there are two major kinds of power: position power and personal power. *Position power* is the power a person derives from a particular office or rank in a formal organizational system. It is the influence capacity a leader derives from having higher status than the followers have. Vice presidents and department heads have more power than staff personnel do because of the positions they hold in the organization. Position power includes legitimate, reward, and coercive power (Table 1-2).

Personal power is the influence capacity a leader derives from being seen by followers as likable and knowledgeable. When leaders act in ways that are important to followers, it gives leaders power. For example, some managers have power because their subordinates consider them to be good role models. Others have power because their subordinates view them as highly competent or considerate. In both cases, these managers' power is ascribed to them by others, based on how they are seen in their relationships with others. Personal power includes referent and expert power (see Table 1-2).

In discussions of leadership, it is not unusual for leaders to be described as wielders of power, as individuals who dominate others. In these instances, power is conceptualized as a tool that leaders use to achieve their own ends. Contrary to this view of power, Burns (1978) emphasized power from a relationship standpoint. For Burns, power is not an entity that leaders use over others to achieve their own ends; instead, power occurs in relationships. It should be used by leaders and followers to promote their collective goals.

In this text, our discussions of leadership treat power as a relational concern for both leaders and followers. We pay attention to how leaders work with followers to reach common goals.

Leadership and Coercion

Coercive power is one of the specific kinds of power available to leaders. Coercion involves the use of force to effect change. *To coerce* means to influence others to do something against their will and may include manipulating penalties and rewards in their work environment. Coercion often involves the use of threats, punishment, and negative reward schedules. Classic examples of coercive leaders are Adolf Hitler in Germany, the Taliban leaders in Afghanistan, Jim Jones in Guyana, and North Korea's Supreme Leader Kim Jong-il, each of whom has used power and restraint to force followers to engage in extreme behaviors.

It is important to distinguish between coercion and leadership because it allows us to separate out from our examples of leadership the behaviors of individuals such as Hitler, the Taliban, and Jones. In our discussions of leadership, coercive people are not used as models of ideal leadership. Our definition suggests that leadership is reserved for those who influence a group of individuals toward a common goal. Leaders who use coercion are interested in their own goals and seldom are interested in the wants and needs of subordinates. Using coercion runs counter to working *with* followers to achieve a common goal.

Leadership and Management

Leadership is a process that is similar to management in many ways. Leadership involves influence, as does management. Leadership entails working with people, which management entails as well. Leadership is concerned with effective goal accomplishment, and so is management. In general, many of the functions of management are activities that are consistent with the definition of leadership we set forth at the beginning of this chapter.

But leadership is also different from management. Whereas the study of leadership can be traced back to Aristotle, management emerged around the turn of the 20th century with the advent of our industrialized society. Management was created as a way to reduce chaos in organizations, to make them run more effectively and efficiently. The primary functions of management, as first identified by Fayol (1916), were planning, organizing, staffing, and controlling. These functions are still representative of the field of management today.

In a book that compared the functions of management with the functions of leadership, Kotter (1990) argued that the functions of the two are quite dissimilar (Figure 1-2). The overriding function of management is to provide order

Management **Produces Order and Consistency**	**Leadership** **Produces Change and Movement**
Planning and Budgeting • Establish agendas • Set timetables • Allocate resources	**Establishing Direction** • Create a vision • Clarify big picture • Set strategies
Organizing and Staffing • Provide structure • Make job placements • Establish rules and procedures	**Aligning People** • Communicate goals • Seek commitment • Build teams and coalitions
Controlling and Problem Solving • Develop incentives • Generate creative solutions • Take corrective action	**Motivating and Inspiring** • Inspire and energize • Empower subordinates • Satisfy unmet needs

SOURCE: Adapted from *A Force for Change: How Leadership Differs From Management* (pp. 3–8), by J. P. Kotter, 1990, New York: Free Press.

Figure 1-2

Functions of Management and Leadership

and consistency to organizations, whereas the primary function of leadership is to produce change and movement. Management is about seeking order and stability; leadership is about seeking adaptive and constructive change.

As illustrated in Figure 1-2, the major activities of management are played out differently than the activities of leadership. Although they are different in scope, Kotter (1990, pp. 7–8) contended that both management and leadership are essential if an organization is to prosper. For example, if an organization has strong management without leadership, the outcome can be stifling and bureaucratic. Conversely, if an organization has strong leadership without management, the outcome can be meaningless or misdirected change for change's sake. To be effective, organizations need to nourish both competent management and skilled leadership.

Many scholars, in addition to Kotter (1990), argue that leadership and management are distinct constructs. For example, Bennis and Nanus (1985) maintained that there is a significant difference between the two. *To manage* means to accomplish activities and master routines, whereas *to lead* means to influence others and create visions for change. Bennis and Nanus made the distinction very clear in their frequently quoted sentence, "Managers are people who do things right and leaders are people who do the right thing" (p. 221).

Rost (1991) has also been a proponent of distinguishing between leadership and management. He contended that leadership is a multidirectional influence relationship and management is a unidirectional authority relationship. Whereas leadership is concerned with the process of developing mutual purposes, management is directed toward coordinating activities in order to get a job done. Leaders and followers work together to create real change, whereas managers and subordinates join forces to sell goods and services (Rost, 1991, pp. 149–152).

Approaching the issue from a narrower viewpoint, Zaleznik (1977) went so far as to argue that leaders and managers themselves are distinct, and that they are basically different types of people. He contended that managers are reactive and prefer to work with people to solve problems but do so with low emotional involvement. They act to limit choices. Zaleznik suggested that leaders, on the other hand, are emotionally active and involved. They seek to shape ideas instead of responding to them and act to expand the available options to solve long-standing problems. Leaders change the way people think about what is possible.

Although there are clear differences between management and leadership, the two constructs overlap. When managers are involved in influencing a group to meet its goals, they are involved in leadership. When leaders are involved in planning, organizing, staffing, and controlling, they are involved in management. Both processes involve influencing a group of individuals toward goal attainment. For purposes of our discussion in this book, we focus on the leadership process. In our examples and case studies, we treat the roles of managers and leaders similarly and do not emphasize the differences between them.

Summary

Leadership is a topic with universal appeal; in the popular press and academic research literature, much has been written about leadership. Despite the abundance of writing on the topic, leadership has presented a major challenge to practitioners and researchers interested in understanding the nature of leadership. It is a highly valued phenomenon that is very complex.

Through the years, leadership has been defined and conceptualized in many ways. The component common to nearly all classifications is that leadership is an influence process that assists groups of individuals toward goal attainment. Specifically, in this book leadership is defined as a process whereby an individual influences a group of individuals to achieve a common goal.

Because both leaders and followers are part of the leadership process, it is important to address issues that confront followers as well as issues that confront leaders. Leaders and followers should be understood in relation to each other.

In prior research, many studies have focused on leadership as a trait. The trait perspective suggests that certain people in our society have special inborn qualities that make them leaders. This view restricts leadership to those who are believed to have special characteristics. In contrast, the approach in this text suggests that leadership is a process that can be learned, and that it is available to everyone.

Two common forms of leadership are *assigned* and *emergent*. *Assigned leadership* is based on a formal title or position in an organization. *Emergent leadership* results from what one does and how one acquires support from followers. Leadership, as a process, applies to individuals in both assigned roles and emergent roles.

Related to leadership is the concept of power, the potential to influence. There are two major kinds of power: position and personal. Position power, which is much like assigned leadership, is the power an individual derives from having a title in a formal organizational system. It includes legitimate, reward, and coercive power. Personal power comes from followers and includes referent and expert power. Followers give it to leaders because followers believe leaders have something of value. Treating power as a shared resource is important because it deemphasizes the idea that leaders are power wielders.

While coercion has been a common power brought to bear by many individuals in charge, it should not be viewed as ideal leadership. Our definition of leadership stresses *using influence* to bring individuals toward a common goal, while coercion involves the use of threats and punishment to *induce change* in followers for the sake of the leaders. Coercion runs counter to leadership because it does not treat leadership as a process that emphasizes working *with* followers to achieve shared objectives.

Leadership and management are different concepts that overlap. They are different in that management traditionally focuses on the activities of planning, organizing, staffing, and controlling, whereas leadership emphasizes the general influence process. According to some researchers, management is concerned with creating order and stability, whereas leadership is about adaptation and constructive change. Other researchers go so far as to argue that managers and leaders are different types of people, with managers being more reactive and less emotionally involved and leaders being more proactive and more emotionally involved. The overlap between leadership and management is centered on how both involve influencing a group of individuals in goal attainment.

In this book, we discuss leadership as a complex process. Based on the research literature, we describe selected approaches to leadership and assess how they can be used to improve leadership in real situations.

References

Bass, B. M. (1990). *Bass and Stogdill's handbook of leadership: A survey of theory and research.* New York: Free Press.

Bennis, W. G., & Nanus, B. (1985). *Leaders: The strategies for taking charge.* New York: Harper & Row.

Bryman, A. (1992). *Charisma and leadership in organizations.* London: Sage.

Bryman, A., Collinson, D., Grint, K., Jackson, G., Uhl-Bien, M. (Eds.). (2011). *The SAGE handbook of leadership.* London, UK: Sage.

Burns, J. M. (1978). *Leadership.* New York: Harper & Row.

Copeland, N. (1942). *Psychology and the soldier.* Harrisburg, PA: Military Service Publications.

Day, D. V., & Antonakis, J. (Eds.). (2012). *The nature of leadership* (2nd ed.). Thousand Oaks, CA: Sage.

Fayol, H. (1916). *General and industrial management.* London: Pitman.

Fisher, B. A. (1974). *Small group decision making: Communication and the group process.* New York: McGraw-Hill.

Fleishman, E. A., Mumford, M. D., Zaccaro, S. J., Levin, K. Y., Korotkin, A. L., & Hein, M. B. (1991). Taxonomic efforts in the description of leader behavior: A synthesis and functional interpretation. *Leadership Quarterly, 2*(4), 245–287.

French, J. R., Jr., & Raven, B. (1959). The bases of social power. In D. Cartwright (Ed.), *Studies in social power* (pp. 259–269). Ann Arbor, MI: Institute for Social Research.

Gardner, J. W. (1990). *On leadership.* New York: Free Press.

Heller, T., & Van Til, J. (1983). Leadership and followership: Some summary propositions. *Journal of Applied Behavioral Science, 18,* 405–414.

Hemphill, J. K. (1949). *Situational factors in leadership.* Columbus: Ohio State University, Bureau of Educational Research.

Hickman, G. R. (Ed.). (2009). *Leading organizations: Perspectives for a new era* (2nd ed.). Thousand Oaks, CA: Sage.

Hogg, M. A. (2001). A social identity theory of leadership. *Personality and Social Psychology Review, 5,* 184–200.

Hollander, E. P. (1992). Leadership, followership, self, and others. *Leadership Quarterly, 3*(1), 43–54.

Jago, A. G. (1982). Leadership: Perspectives in theory and research. *Management Science, 28*(3), 315–336.

Kotter, J. P. (1990). *A force for change: How leadership differs from management.* New York: Free Press.

Moore, B. V. (1927). The May conference on leadership. *Personnel Journal, 6,* 124–128.

Mumford, M. D. (2006). *Pathways to outstanding leadership: A comparative analysis of charismatic, ideological, and pragmatic leaders.* Mahwah, NJ: Lawrence Erlbaum.

Peters, T. J., & Waterman, R. H. (1982). *In search of excellence: Lessons from America's best-run companies.* New York: Warner Books.

Rost, J. C. (1991). *Leadership for the twenty-first century.* New York: Praeger.

Seeman, M. (1960). *Social status and leadership.* Columbus: Ohio State University, Bureau of Educational Research.

Smith, J. A., & Foti, R. J. (1998). A pattern approach to the study of leader emergence. *Leadership Quarterly, 9*(2), 147–160.

Stogdill, R. M. (1974). *Handbook of leadership: A survey of theory and research.* New York: Free Press.

Watson, C., & Hoffman, L. R. (2004). The role of task-related behavior in the emergence of leaders. *Group & Organization Management, 29*(6), 659–685.

Zaleznik, A. (1977, May–June). Managers and leaders: Are they different? *Harvard Business Review, 55,* 67–78.

chapter 2

The Relational Leadership Model

by Susan R. Komives, Nance Lucas, and Timothy R. McMahon

In the previous chapter, we reviewed how theorists' view of leadership has changed, from the belief that leaders are simply born to the idea that the best way to learn about leadership is to study the behaviors or practices of people who are viewed as leaders. Theorizing has evolved even further into an understanding of leadership as a complex process. Indeed, leadership is a transforming process that raises all participants to levels at which they can become effective leaders.

Leadership may best be understood as philosophy. At its core, understanding philosophy means understanding values. "Affect, motives, attitudes, beliefs, values, ethics, morals, will, commitment, preferences, norms, expectations, responsibilities—such are the concerns of leadership philosophy proper. Their study is paramount because the very nature of leadership is that of practical philosophy, philosophy-in-action" (Hodgkinson, 1983, p. 202). When we examine historical leaders, we often are analyzing the values and ethics that characterized their leadership. It is critical that we each develop our own personal philosophy—one we hope will include the elements of the model presented in this chapter.

Chapter Overview

This chapter presents a relational model of leadership to consider in building your own personal philosophy. Each of the elements of the model is presented in detail to give you more information about each component.

Relational Leadership

Leadership has to do with relationships, the role of which cannot be overstated. Leadership is inherently a relational, communal process. "Leadership is always dependent on the context, but the context is established by the relationships we value" (Wheatley, 1992, p. 144). Although a person could exert leadership of ideas through persuasive writings or making speeches, most leadership happens in an interactive context between individuals and among group members. We emphasize once again: we view leadership as *a relational and ethical process of people together attempting to accomplish positive change.*

Leadership theories and models have changed over time. These changing frameworks are reflected in the descriptive terms that have been affixed to the word *leadership.* Examples of these leadership theories and concepts include situational, transforming, servant-leadership, authentic leadership, and principle-centered leadership. We have used the term *relational leadership* as a reminder that relationships are the focal point of the leadership process.

Relational leadership involves a focus on five primary components. This approach to leadership is purposeful and builds commitment toward positive purposes that are inclusive of people and diverse points of view, empowers those involved, is ethical, and recognizes that all four of these elements are accomplished by being process-oriented.

The model provides a frame of reference or an approach to leadership in contemporary organizations. With these foundational philosophies and com-

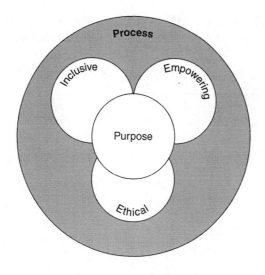

Figure 2-1

Relational Leadership
Model

mitments, an individual can make a meaningful contribution in any organization. This model is not a leadership theory in itself, and it does not address the change outcomes for which leadership is intended. The Relational Leadership Model does not seek to describe the way leadership is currently practiced in all groups or organizations, but is an aspirational model that we propose in developing and supporting a healthy, ethical, effective group. It is a framework connecting five key elements that can serve as a responsive approach to leadership. Figure 2-1 offers a visual image of the elements of the model.

The components of relational leadership are complex concepts. Think about your own level of comfort or knowledge about each component as you read the related dimensions of each element. The model reflects how the organization's or community's purpose influences the components of being inclusive, empowering, and ethical. For example, the purpose of the Habitat for Humanity Club on campus is to engage its members to assist in providing houses for those who cannot afford them on their own. The purpose includes others, empowers them to use their leadership and talents to make a difference, and is ethical in that it benefits others and improves the quality of life in a community. How that purpose is achieved (the process) is just as important as the outcome. How the goals are accomplished and how others are involved in the process matters in the leadership process. The purpose is vision-driven and not position-driven. Leaders and members promote the organization's purpose through a shared vision and not for self-gain such as achieving a higher leadership position or fame.

Exhibit 2-1 identifies some important knowledge, attitudes, and skills that are embedded in each element. These reflect the knowledge, attitudes, and skills that would be helpful in understanding relational leadership. Brief applications of the core elements to the knowing-being-doing model conclude each section. For example, in order to practice inclusiveness, you must

- Know yourself and others; engage yourself in learning new information as you develop the competencies required in your role (knowledge)
- Be open to difference and value other perspectives (attitudes)
- Practice listening skills, coalition building, interpersonal skills, and effective civil discourse (skills)

Exhibit 2-1   Relational Leadership Model Compared to Knowing–Being–Doing

Leadership Component	Knowing (Knowledge and Understanding)	Being (Attitudes)	Doing (Skills)
Purposeful	How change occurs Core elements of change Role of mission or vision Shared values Common purpose	Hopeful Committed "Can do" attitude Likes improvement Commitment to social responsibility	Identifying goals Envisioning Meaning-making Creative thinking Involving others in vision-building process
Inclusive	Self and others Citizenship Frames and multiple realities	Open to difference Values equity Web-like thinking Believes everyone can make a difference	Talent development Listening skills Building coalitions Framing and reframing Civil discourse
Empowering	Power How policies or procedures block or promote empowerment Personal mastery Control is not possible	Believes each has something to offer Self-esteem Concern for others' growth Values others' contributions Willing to share power	Gate-keeping skills Sharing information Individual and team learning Encouraging or affirming others Capacity building Promoting self-leadership Practicing renewal
Ethical	How values develop How systems influence justice and care Self and others' values Ethical decision-making models	Commitment to socially responsible behavior Confronting behavior Values integrity Trustworthy Authentic Establishes sense of personal character Responsible Expects high standards Puts benefit to others over self-gain	Being congruent Being trusting Being reliable Having courage Using moral imagination
Process-Oriented	Community Group process Relational aspect of leadership Process is as important as outcomes	Values process as well as outcomes Quality effort Develops systems perspective	Collaboration Reflection Meaning making Challenge Civil confrontation Learning Giving and receiving feedback

Knowing-Being-Doing

Individuals involved in the leadership process (leaders, members, co-creators, and so on) need to know themselves well before they can effectively work with others to influence change or achieve common purpose. It is not enough to simply drive an agenda or accomplish small or big wins. The leadership process calls for those engaged in it to be knowledgeable (knowing), to be aware of self and others (being), and to act (doing). The knowing-being-doing model represents a holistic approach to the leadership development of yourself and others. These three components are interrelated—the knowledge you possess can influence your ways of thinking, which can influence your actions. And it is also true that your beliefs and way of existing in this world (being) can influence your actions, which can influence your behaviors. This pattern of influence is circular and not on a straight path.

Other ways to view this holistic approach is by using the framework of knowledge, skills, and attitudes or head, heart, and practice. Palmer (1998) uses the phrase "head, heart, and practice" to describe the paradoxes in teaching and what happens when we keep the head (knowing and intellect) separated from the heart (being) and even further separated from practice (doing). Palmer argues that we need a synthesis of all three components in the teaching process. The same applies in the leadership process.

The Army coined the phrase "know, be, do." People will collaborate with those who are credible (both leaders and members)—those who are knowing. Leaders need to demonstrate competence and maintain a certain amount of knowledge. Hesselbein and Shinseki (2004) offer four levels of skills essential to leadership: interpersonal skills, conceptual skills (ability to think creatively), technical skills (expertise required for position), and tactical skills (negotiation, human relations, and other skills necessary to achieve objectives) (p. 12). Knowing is an ongoing process that allows leaders to continue to develop, learn, and grow.

In the Army, the "be" means knowing what values and attributes define you as a leader (Hesselbein & Shinseki, 2004). "Your character helps you know what is right; more than that, it links that knowledge to action. Character gives you the courage to do what is right regardless of the circumstances or consequences" (p. 11). The Army's acronym of leadership is LDRSHIP: Loyalty, Duty, Respect, Selfless service, Honor, Integrity, Personal courage (p. 11). That is the essence of the "be" of leadership. Lao Tzu offers another example of being. This Eastern reflection of having a sense of self and being centered in self-awareness is important to relating well with others.

The "doing" of knowing and being means acting. Character and knowledge are not enough in facilitating change in the leadership process. Doing attempts to produce results, accomplishes the vision, creates change, and influences others to act. Sometimes leaders will fail to act because of indecision or due to a fixation on perfection. "Competent, confident leaders tolerate honest mistakes that are not the result of negligence. A leader who sets a standard of 'zero defects, no mistakes' is also saying, 'Don't take any chances'" (Hesselbein & Shinseki, 2004, p. 15).

Learning is an outcome of the knowing-being-doing developmental model or feedback system. Be attuned to how new learning is changing your attitudes and behaviors or is changing you in general. It is important to reflect upon how and what you are learning as you go through those cycles. "Leaders promote learning in at least three ways: through their own learning on a personal level, by helping others in their units [organizations] learn, and by shaping and contributing to an organizational culture that promotes learning" (Hesselbein & Shinseki, 2004, p. 133).

As you continue reading this and the following chapters, consider how this model is adding to your knowledge. How can you take this information and incorporate it into your beliefs surrounding leadership? What actions can you take with this new knowledge? Consciously examining your thoughts, feelings, and actions allows you to continue to learn and grow both as a leader and as a human being.

Relational Leadership Is Purposeful

Being purposeful means having a commitment to a goal or activity. It is also the ability to collaborate and to find common ground with others to facilitate positive change. Creating positive change can mean working hard toward resolving differences among participants, finding a common direction, and building a shared vision to improve the organization or enhance others in some way. Even if a participant does not have a vision, that person knows enough to ask others, "Remind me what we are working toward. What do we all hope will happen?" Trusting the process, several in the group will chime in with their ideas, and someone will have the talent to express those words in terms of the vision and purpose that will bring nods of agreement from nearly every person present. It is important that all group members be able to articulate that purpose and use it as a driving force. That is an essential element in relational leadership.

The conventional paradigm of leadership often asserts that the positional leader must have a clear vision. Research, however, has shown two primary types of vision activity: personalized vision and socialized vision (Howell, 1988). Personalized vision refers to a person, usually the person with legitimate authority, announcing a dream or plan and imposing it on others. Participants seem to have little choice and must adopt this vision, which results in varying degrees of personal ownership or commitment. Jack Welch, the former CEO of General Electric (GE), is an excellent example of an authoritative leader with a personalized vision. Although Jack Welch was a strong leader with a public presence, he did not single-handedly raise the profile of GE. Even though Jack Welch had the legitimate power to do so, it did not automatically ensure commitment from his employees. He started his tenure as CEO as a commanding leader and then, over time, developed a more humanistic leadership approach that inspired GE's employees with a values-based vision (O'Toole, 2003).

Socialized vision is building a vision from among group members, recognizing that people support what they help create. Sharing vision does not mean that each person must create and possess a vision, but that each person must be involved in the process of building a vision with others. "Effective leaders don't just impose their vision on others, they recruit others to a shared vision. Especially in our digital age, when power tends to coalesce around ideas, not position, leadership is a partnership, not a sinecure" (Bennis & Thomas, 2002, p. 137). Think about your personality preferences. Do you think creatively and see possibilities in everything, or are you shaking your head right now, thinking "No way!" Do you have ideas about your future and a vision of how things might be? Such a vision is a picture of "a realistic, credible, attractive future" for yourself or your organization (Nanus, 1992, p. 8).

After hearing a presentation on empowering leadership and the importance of shared vision, one of our colleagues approached the presenter. She said, "I just am not creative or cannot articulate a vision. I am practical and realistic. I feel capable but am more of a maintainer than a builder. I can keep things going more than I am able to think them up in the first place." The first piece of advice that organization consultant Burt Nanus (1992) shares with those trying to avoid failures in organizational vision is, "Don't do it alone" (p. 167).

Being purposeful with a group vision that includes a positive change effort helps you set priorities and make decisions congruent with that dream. "Vision animates, inspirits, and transforms purpose into action" (Bennis & Goldsmith, 1994, p. 101). This action component to vision is described well by the engraving in an eighteenth-century church in Sussex, England:

A vision without a task is but a dream,
a task without a vision is drudgery,
a vision and a task
is the hope of the world.

(From Transcultural Leadership, *p. 106, by G. F. Simons, C. Vázquez, & P. R. Harris. Copyright © 1993, with permission from Elsevier.)*

"To be motivating, a vision must be a source of self-esteem and common purpose. . . . The core of the vision is the organization's mission statement, which describes the general purpose of the organization" (Yukl, 1989, p. 336). One approach that is used by executives to develop shared visions is an exercise involving magazine articles. Organizational members are asked to identify their favorite magazine or a magazine closely related to the organization's purpose and write a feature story that will describe the organization in the future (four or five years from the present time) using headlines (Yukl). This powerful activity allows everyone to dream together and to begin the visioning process using creativity, imagination, and passion.

Your individual, purposeful commitment to the shared vision of a group project means you will do your part, share resources, and support your teammates because you expect the same of them. Vision guides action. "It's not what a vision is, it's what a vision does" (Kazuo Inamori, as cited in Senge, 1990, p. 207). A vision of a homecoming weekend reaching the broadest possible group of alumni will guide all the committee's choices about how to diversify that event.

"Success can be measured in many ways such as reaching your goal, involving new groups or individuals with new perspectives, and creating awareness or change. In the organizations I have been involved with, success has come by including those who are highly motivated and want to make a difference and have a clear understanding of the goal to be achieved. When this happens, it becomes easier to accomplish tasks because everyone is working towards the same goal. It is beneficial to utilize special groups or individuals who have expertise on your project to gain new insight, help motivate others, and provide additional resources and support."—Brynn DeLong is a member of the Blue Chip Leadership Program and majors in political science at the University of Arizona.

A vision inspires energy and purpose. Retired General Norman Schwarzkopf observed, "I have found that in order to be a leader, you are almost serving a cause" (Wren, 1994, p. 4). Purposeful participants have emotionally identified with a purpose and a dream. "There is no more powerful engine driving an organization toward excellence and long-range success than an attractive, worthwhile, and achievable vision of the future, widely shared" (Nanus, 1992, p. 3).

Working for Positive Change

One common purpose that pulls people together is working toward change. Change processes can have various motives associated with them. The Relational Leadership Model supports positive change—that is, change that improves the human condition and that does not intentionally harm others. The antithesis of this is facilitating change that is destructive, like the attacks on the World Trade Center in New York City. When facilitating a positive change process, the means justify the ends.

Rost (1991) proposes that leadership happens when the group *intends* to accomplish change, not just when they *do* accomplish change. Having the intention of improving a situation, accomplishing a task, or implementing a common purpose is part of the change process. Change may not happen for many reasons, but the core fact that the group intended to make a difference is central. John Parr (1994), president of the National Civic League, writes, "Positive change can occur when people with different perspectives are organized into groups in which everyone is regarded as a peer. There must be a high level of involvement, a clear purpose, adequate resources, and the power to decide and implement" (p. xiii).

Some situations are profoundly hard to change. It is hard to move away from the status quo—the way things are. Change theory proposes that change often begins when something unfreezes a situation. The cycle is often presented as unfreezing → changing → refreezing. This "unfreezing" may be caused by a trigger event, such as a carjacking in a remote campus parking lot, a campus riot following a sporting event, or a disappointingly small attendance at a group's expensive activity. People pay attention to the problem with a focus they did not have prior to the incident. Unfreezing may also occur when external policies change—when a new law is enacted, for example. Unfreezing makes it possible to address an issue or policy that has not commanded the attention of those who need to address it. The change process is then engaged and the issue is addressed.

Even after a change is implemented, it would be an error in these times even to consider any issue "refrozen." Instead, it is best to consider the outcome to be "slush," so that the solution is seen not as final but as permeable and open to be readdressed easily. It may be best to consider solutions as automatically open for review, regularly evaluated, and flexible. The classic change model (Lewin, 1958), describing the change process as moving from the present state through a transition state to a desired state, still works, but we encourage a caution that the desired state should now be viewed as less rigid.

Change can be thought of as moving some situation away from the status quo to a different place. To understand why that movement is hard, examine the driving forces pushing for change and the resisting forces striving to keep change from happening to preserve the status quo. Clearly, not all change is appropriate or supportable. When it is, the driving forces working toward change should be enhanced and the restraining forces minimized. This "force-field analysis" is a useful method for identifying aspects of the situation that could enhance change (Lippitt, 1969, p. 157).

Kotter and Cohen (2002) refer to the concept of "removing barriers in the mind" as another reason why people are resistant to change or to changing. "After years of stability, incremental change, or failed attempts at change, people can internalize a deep belief that they are not capable of achieving a leap. They may not say out loud 'I can't do it,' but at some level they feel it, even when it is not true" (p. 112). It is important to understand that the mind can both disempower and empower individuals toward change.

We are constantly faced with the dynamic tension of how things are and how we think they ought to be. This "is-ought" dichotomy asks us to face reality but work toward true transformative change, real change—to move toward the more hopeful vision. This "creative tension" brings energy to the change effort (Senge, 1990, p. 150). Connecting personal hopes and commitments to a group vision is a creative process. This process can be time-consuming. When a group is newly formed, the process of building a group vision can be energetic and hopeful if the group quickly comes to agreement and commitment, or it can be anxious and cautious if the group shows little agreement. When joining an ongoing group in which a vision has already been established, new participants have to determine whether they can connect to that vision or feel they can help shape the continued evolution of the group's vision over time.

Relational Leadership Is Inclusive

Being inclusive means understanding, valuing, and actively engaging diversity in views, approaches, styles, and aspects of individuality, such as sex or culture, that add multiple perspectives to a group's activity. As a foundation for valuing inclusion, you will have a chance to explore your own attitudes and attributes and examine those of others. Exhibit 2-1 highlights aspects of being inclusive to illustrate how you might explore this component. It means understanding how different groups or individuals might approach issues from different perspectives or frames, maintaining the attitudes that respect differences, and valuing equity and involvement. It means thinking of networks and webs of connection instead of seeing issues and problems as isolated and discrete. Being inclusive embraces having the skills to develop the talent of members so they can be readily involved. Listening with empathy and communicating with civility are communication skills that facilitate the inclusion of others. Inclusiveness breeds new leadership and creates a positive cycle that sustains the quality of an organization over time.

Although many things seem unpredictable and even unconnected, there is unity in nature; seemingly unrelated parts influence each other as well as the whole. By applying these concepts to the leadership world, we learn to understand that the group or organization represents unity or wholeness built from and influenced greatly by the smallest subunits of that system. "As we move away from viewing the organization as a complex of parts and deal with it as a unity, then problems met in leadership can make more sense and solutions become obvious" (Fairholm, 1994, p. 59).

Individuals are important because they concurrently represent and influence the whole. The purpose, vision, and values of the whole come to life as each individual member describes and applies them. The goal is not to overcome the variations and differences among participants—indeed, those variations bring creativity and energy—but to build shared purpose. "Leading others to lead themselves is the key to tapping the intelligence, the spirit, the creativity, the commitment, and most of all, the tremendous, unique potential of each individual" (Manz & Sims, 1989, p. 225).

> "When, as a leader, you are able to empower others and create a sense of community among members, everyone will be compelled to contribute their unique talents. The group will then meet its potential to fulfill its purpose."—Gina Pagel is a volunteer for the American Cancer Society Relay for Life and the president of the Student Wisconsin Education Association Chapter at Edgewood College.

Being inclusive means developing the strengths and talent of group members so they can contribute to the group's goals.

> Leaders enhance the learning of others, helping them to develop their own initiative, strengthening them in the use of their own judgment, and enabling them to grow and to become better contributors to the organization. These leaders, by virtue of their learning, then become leaders and mentors to others. (McGill & Slocum, 1993, p. 11)

It is not sufficient just to be a participative leader involving group members in the work of the organization. Organizations have to go further and recognize that in many cases the organizational culture has to change to effectively involve people who have different backgrounds and different views and who may not embrace the dominant cultural norms. In addition to its practice, the language of inclusivity is exceptionally important. How we talk about people in the organization, how we refer to them (colleagues versus subordinates or participants versus followers), and how the organization is structured are indicators of inclusive environments (Hesselbein, 2002). Think about the message being sent by using the word *we* instead of the word *I*. You might engage in a conversation with someone and hear an excessive use of the word *I* from that person. What impression did that individual make on you? Did you feel engaged in the conversation? Hesselbein describes the model of inclusion best by stating, from her own experiences,

> Building the inclusive, cohesive, vibrant institution does indeed require the biggest basket in town—for it has to have room for all of us. Not just the favored few, those who look alike and think alike, but all who are part of the community of the future. When equal access prevails, the synergy of inclusion propels us far beyond the old gated enclaves of the past into the richness of opportunities that lie beyond the walls. (p. 20)

Groups would benefit by examining practices that might block inclusivity. A group might be so accustomed to voting on every decision that it has alienated members who find this process uncomfortable. Those members might like to use a consensus model of decision making to ensure that the views of all are included in each significant decision. For example, the extreme use of Robert's Rules of Order has the potential to cut off discussion when issues are unresolved and the direction is unclear. Another illustration is when a student union program committee traditionally provides music or movies of interest to only one segment of the campus. They would need to examine that practice and involve others with different interests in order to diversify programming. Organizational practices, such as always meeting at 9 P.M., might exclude the involvement of people such as adult learners and those who cannot be on campus at that time because of family or work obligations, or because commuting is a problem. When the group realizes, for example, that no commuter students, or students of color, or men are involved in their activities, that should be a signal that something is wrong. Other ways of communicating and consulting with people should be found, as should other ways of including diverse interests in group decision making.

Involving Those External to the Group

Being inclusive also means identifying the shareholders and stakeholders external to the group who have some responsibility (a share) or interest (a stake) in the change that is being planned. It would be exclusive, not inclusive, for a group to assume that they should or could accomplish a major change alone. For example, an organization like the Latino Student Union might seek to change a campus practice about how scholarship programs are advertised to new Latino students. Being inclusive means the Latino Student Union should also consider which other campus groups or offices might be stakeholders in resolving this issue because they have a shared interest or could be affected by the consequences of any action (Bryson & Crosby, 1992). The Latino Student Union might then reach out to form coalitions or some involvement with such groups as the Council of Black Fraternity and Sorority Chapters, the Black Student Union, the Multicultural Affairs Committee of the Student Government Association, and other related student organizations like the Honors Program. In addition, the Latino Student Union should identify the shareholders in resolving the issue—the Financial Aid Office, the Dean of Students Office, and the Office of Minority Affairs. These offices would each want to get the word out to students about their programs and need not be thought of as negative or antagonistic to the changes. They might in fact appreciate help in resolving problems they too experience in the current process.

Stakeholders may not all hold the same view of a problem, and they may not all seek the same solutions. Bryson and Crosby (1992) clarify how a stakeholder's position on an issue (ranging from high support to high opposition) is influenced by the importance with which they view the issue (ranging from least important to most important). This makes stakeholders' responses more understandable (see Figure 2-2). As they work toward being more inclusive, relational leaders will want to assess possible stakeholder reactions in determining their approaches.

Perspective or stand on the issues

Degree of importance to the stakeholder	High Opposition	High Support
High Importance	Antagonistic	Supportive
Low Importance	Problematic	Low Priority

Figure 2-2

Responses of Stakeholders to Shared Issues and Goals.

SOURCE: Adapted from Bryson & Crosby (1992), p. 268. Used with permission.

Even if stakeholders disagree on an issue, they should be involved. Involvement helps stakeholders gain new views on issues and may build support among various stakeholders toward an intended change. They also bring in an outside viewpoint, which contributes to the overall knowledge of the group. Stakeholders might see dimensions of an issue that the group is blind to. Building support and forming coalitions are related skills for relational leaders.

Relational Leadership Is Empowering

"Thriving on change demands the empowerment of every person in the organization—no ifs, ands, or buts" (Peters, 1989, p. xiv). Empowerment has two dimensions: (1) the sense of self that claims ownership, claims a place in the process, and expects to be involved, and (2) a set of environmental conditions (in the group or organization) that promote the full involvement of participants by reducing the barriers that block the development of individual talent and involvement. Empowerment is claimed ("I have a legitimate right to be here and say what I feel and think") as well as shared with others ("You should be involved in this; you have a right to be here too; tell us what you think and feel"). Being empowering means mitigating aspects of the environmental climate that can block meaningful involvement for others. Empowering environments are learning climates in which people expect successes yet know they can learn from failures or mistakes. It is important to establish organizational environments that empower others to do and to be their best.

The root word in the concept of empowerment is *power*. Understanding power dynamics is essential in moving toward a philosophical commitment to empowerment. Where possible, positional leaders must be willing to share their power or authority, and participants must be willing to assume more responsibility for group outcomes. Power has traditionally been viewed on a zero-sum basis. Conventional approaches assumed that if one person in an organization is very powerful, then someone else has less power. In truth, different types of power exist concurrently among people in any kind of relationship. Power dynamics range from power "over" (autocratic approaches) to power "with" (collaborative approaches) or power "alongside" (collegial approaches). Some approaches to leadership would go further and describe power "from," referring to the authority and power afforded to a leader from a group of participants. Effective positional leaders know that their power and ability to be effective comes from the members of their group—their participants (Kouzes & Posner, 1987).

Sources of Power

How a person uses power and reacts to the power of others must be examined in relational leadership. In their classic work, French and Raven (1959) identify five primary sources of power that individuals bring to their relationships with others. These bases of social power are expert power, referent power, legitimate power, coercive power, and reward power.

Expert power is the power of information or knowledge. Expertise may come through professional development and formal education (such as that received by engineers or dentists), from possessing specific information (such as remembering the results of a recent survey or knowing the rules in the student handbook), or from extended experience (such as being the mother of three children or being a seasoned baseball player). We trust experts and give them power over us based on their assumed higher level of knowledge or experience.

Referent power refers to the nature and strength of a relationship between two or more people. Think of the wise senior who is so highly regarded that her words carry great weight in the group discussion.

Legitimate power is due to the formal role a person holds, usually because he or she has the responsibility and authority to exert some degree of power. For instance, the president of a student organization has power to make certain decisions due to the nature of his or her role. However, those in authority generally know that their legitimate power is fragile.

Coercive power influences individuals or groups through imposing or threatening punitive sanctions or removing rewards or benefits. Coercion accomplishes behavior change but usually at great cost to the relationships among those involved. Because leadership is an influence relationship, it is essential that this influence be "noncoercive" (Rost, 1993, p. 105).

Conversely, reward power influences behavior through the ability to deliver positive outcomes and desired resources. Rewards may be extrinsic, like raises, plaques, or special privileges. They may also be intrinsic—intangibles like praise or support.

You may intentionally use some source of power. For example, you might prepare very well before a meeting so you will be an expert on some topic. Conversely, others may attribute some source of power to you without your knowing what is happening, as, for example, when someone fears your disapproval because you have referent power. To empower ourselves and others, it is essential to understand power.

Understanding Power

In many cases, we give power away. We do it when we do not trust our own opinion if it contradicts that of an expert. We assume the expert knows more. Yet when the doctor too readily concludes that you just need bed rest and you know it's something more serious, you should insist that your doctor explore other alternatives. When the person with legitimate power announces a plan or an approach, we give power away if we do not say, "We would like to talk about that first because we might have some additional ideas that would be helpful." We may also have power attributed to us that is undeserved. When the group assumes that because you are an English major you would be best at writing the group's report, they may be in error.

Power is not finite and indeed can be shared and amplified. Some think that power should be framed differently and seen with a similar frame as love: the more you give away, the more you get. If the leadership paradigm of your colleagues is very conventional, they may see the sharing of power as indecisiveness or an avoidance of responsibility. Others may abuse the power shared with them, but those in legitimate authority roles who share their power usually find that they build stronger groups.

For the society to get its work done, leaders and the systems over which they preside must be granted some measure of power. It is a common experience for leaders today to have far less power than they need to accomplish the tasks that we hand them. They must have the power to get results (Gardner, 2003, p. 201).

Gardner goes on to say that those who hold power must be held account-able. Leaders are in a greater position of power when they hold themselves accountable first before waiting for others to implement a system of checks and balances.

Hoarding power in leadership risks negative responses from others, such as sabotage, withdrawal, resistance, anger, and other behaviors that would contra-dict the positive goals and objectives of the group. "The key gift that leaders can offer is power" (Bolman & Deal, 2003a, p. 341). When people can use and hear their voices in the life of an organization or community, they will feel a sense of justice and a belief that they matter.

Self-Empowerment

Empowerment is claiming the power you should have from any position in the organization. Self-empowerment then is the recognition that you have a legiti-mate right to be heard and the self-confidence to be part of a solution or the change process. "The E-word by itself, is a non sequitur unless it's used with self-discovery . . . it provides a means of empowering yourself as you explore your natural, educational, and professional attributes in sizing up your leadership prospects" (Haas & Tamarkin, 1992, p. 35). Murrell (1985, pp. 36–37) presents six methods through which you might become empowered:

1. Educating (discovering/sharing information and knowledge)
2. Leading (inspiring, rewarding, directing)
3. Structuring (creating structural factors such as arranging your day, bringing people to the table, changing policies or processes so that they change lives beyond the people who created it)
4. Providing (making sure others have resources to get their job done)
5. Mentoring (having close personal relationships)
6. Actualizing (taking it on—being empowered—claiming it)

Valuing the empowerment of all members creates a larger group of partici-pants or citizens who generally take more ownership of group tasks and processes and who feel committed to the outcomes of the change.

Mattering and Marginality

Empowerment places you at the center of what is happening rather than at the edges, where you might feel inconsequential. This may be understood best by examining the concepts of mattering and marginality. Schlossberg (1989b) has extended and applied the work of sociologist Morris Rosenberg on mattering to her own work in studying adults in transition. "Mattering is a motive: the feeling that others depend on us, are interested in us, are concerned with our fate . . . [which] exercises a powerful influence on our actions" (Rosenberg & McCul-lough, as cited in Schlossberg, 1989b, p. 8). In new situations, in new roles, or with new people, we may feel marginal, as if we do not matter unless the group welcomes us and seeks our meaningful involvement. In contrast, mattering is the feeling that we are significant to others and to the process. Think of the anxiety and perhaps marginalization of potential new members coming to their first meeting of the Campus Environmental Coalition—or any group. They could be scarcely noticed, become isolated, and perhaps be ignored, or they could be welcomed, involved, and engaged, and know that they matter. Think about the positive feelings imparted to a first-year student when an upper-class veteran of an organization requests his or her opinion on an issue.

Empowering Environments

Groups, organizations, or environments can promote mattering or can keep people on the periphery—in the margins. We need environments that promote the development of the human spirit on a local scale, thus creating a "fundamental shift of mind, in which individuals come to see themselves as capable of creating the world they truly want rather than merely reacting to circumstances beyond their control" (Kiefer & Senge, 1984, p. 68).

Empowerment is likely to happen in organizational environments where people recognize that things can always be better than they are now. These organizations expect to learn and seek new solutions. Empowering organizations seek to eliminate fear or humiliation and operate on trust and inclusivity. If you do not feel empowered in a particular group, you might assess the dynamics in the organization to see if they are encouraging or controlling. There may be an in-group and an out-group, and those in the out-group are excluded from access to information and opportunities to shape decisions (Kohn, 1992). If the organizational dynamics are basically supportive, however, perhaps you need to enhance your self-empowerment by building competencies, networks, or attributes to let you make a meaningful contribution.

Empowerment and delegation are not the same thing. A leader cannot give tasks to participants to do, no matter how important those assignments may be, and simply assume that participants will subsequently feel empowered. Indeed, if the leader retains a great deal of power or control when delegating, participants may feel manipulated, unprepared, resentful, or victimized. Conversely, if a positional leader has clearly acted congruently in sharing authority and responsibility with the group and has its trust, then sharing tasks can be empowering and can enhance community. Empowerment is achieved by enabling the involvement of group members and conveying faith in them.

"I was recently elected President of the Executive Board at Endicott College, after residing as Vice President of my class for a year. The role of the executive board is to organize and run the Student Government Association (SGA). As the new Executive President, I plan to make some changes in the organization of the SGA. I am planning on making more class officers be involved in the activities and events run by the SGA. I aspire to make everyone feel as though they have a significant role in every issue that comes across SGA's path. I believe when people feel that they are important they realize their potential. They also realize that when contributing to a greater whole, much personal satisfaction is gained. Once an individual is given the chance to take action and lead, they become more involved and dedicated on their own thereafter because they realize what they are accomplishing makes such a difference to the community."—Elyse Goldstein is vice president of the class of 2007 at Endicott College and a student curator of the David Broudo Gallery.

Relational Leadership Is Ethical

A seven-year-old goes into the grocery store with his father. Upon arriving home, the father discovers that little Johnny has a pocketful of candy that was not a part of the purchase. Horrified at Johnny's stealing, the father demands that Johnny return the candy to the store, confess to the store manager, apologize for his behavior, and promise never to steal from any store again. For some of us, an incident like this was our first real lesson in what is good and what is bad, what is virtuous and what is immoral. Early in our lives, in lessons such as this one, we were taught to value honesty over dishonesty, kindness over cruelty, and doing the right thing over breaking the law.

Ethical and Moral Leadership

The Relational Leadership Model emphasizes ethical and moral leadership, meaning leadership that is driven by values and standards and leadership that is good—moral—in nature. The language we use to examine ethical, moral leadership is of utmost importance. Some have a tendency to use the terms *ethics* and *morals* interchangeably (Henderson, 1992; Walton, 1988). Others differentiate between them, yet draw a strong relationship between ethics and morals (Shea, 1988). Shaw and Barry (1989) define ethics as "the social rules that govern and limit our conduct, especially the ultimate rules concerning right and wrong" (pp. 2–3).

The derivation of ethics is from *ethos*, from the Greek words for "character" and "sentiment of the community" (Toffler, 1986, p. 10). Other definitions of ethics include "the principles of conduct governing an individual or a profession" and "standards of behavior" (Shea, 1988, p. 17). Being ethical means "conforming to the standards of a given profession or group. Any group can set its own ethical standards and then live by them or not" (Toffler, 1986, p. 10). Ethical standards, whether they are established by an individual or an organization, help guide a person's decisions and actions. For the purposes of this model, ethics will be defined as "rules or standards that govern behaviors" (Toffler, 1986, p. 10).

Stephen Covey, author of the best-selling book *The 7 Habits of Highly Effective People* (1989), uses the metaphor of "leadership by compass" to illustrate principle-centered leadership (p. 19). Principles, like values, ethics, standards, and morals, "provide 'true north' direction to our lives when navigating the 'streams' of our environments" (p. 19).

Professions often establish codes of ethics or standards that serve as normative expectations for people in a particular profession. Lawyers must adhere to the American Bar Association's code of ethics for attorneys, and the American Medical Association promotes a code of ethics for physicians. Every McDonald's restaurant prominently displays a code of standards that pledges excellence in its food and service. Upon closer examination, these organizations are promoting standards by which they expect professionals and employees to live.

Moral means "relating to principles of right and wrong" (Toffler, 1986, p. 10) or "arising from one's conscience or a sense of good and evil; pertaining to the discernment of good and evil; instructive of what is good or evil (bad)" (Shea, 1988, p. 17). Morals are commonly thought to be influenced by religion or personal beliefs. Moral leadership is concerned with "good" leadership; that is, leadership with good means and good ends.

Our philosophy of leadership is values-driven. Again, our definition underscores this: *leadership is a relational and ethical process of people together attempting to accomplish positive change.* Using this philosophy, leaders and followers act out of a sense of shared values—the desire to cause real change and a commitment to mutual purposes. The actions of leaders and participants emanate from a set of values, which we hope are congruent and shared. Values are "freely chosen personal beliefs" (Lewis, 1990, p. 9) or the "guiding principles in our lives with respect to the personal and social ends we desire" (Kouzes & Posner, 1993, p. 60). Simply stated, values are our personal beliefs.

Although there is much disagreement in the leadership literature over definitions and theory, and about whether leadership is values-neutral or values-driven, it is safe to say that most people expect leaders to do the right thing. In a 1988 Gallup poll of 1,200 workers and managers, 89% of the respondents "believed it was important for leaders to be upright, honest, and ethical in their dealings" (Hughes, Ginnett, & Curphy, 1993, p. 170). Unfortunately, only 41% of those surveyed believed that their supervisor exhibited these qualities (Hughes et al.). A 2003 Gallup Poll on Governance found that only 53% of those surveyed had "a great deal" or "a fair amount" of trust in the government of their state (Jones, 2003, p. 1). Trust in state governments has declined since the events of September 11, 2001. Securing and keeping the trust of your constituencies is central to leadership. When 1,500 executives from 20 countries were asked what the requirements were for an ideal chief corporate officer, personal ethics was ranked at the top of the list (Kidder, 1993). A Gallup Youth Survey conducted in 2003 revealed that 67% of youth between the ages of 13 and 17 reported "a great deal" to "a fair amount" of cheating in their schools, with half of them indicating that they also cheated (Kidder, 2005, p. 267).

As leaders and citizens, our challenge today is to close the gap between our expectations of ethical leadership and the reality of frequent breaches of ethical conduct by our leaders. We need bold, courageous leadership—leadership that is by word and deed ethical and moral. It is encouraging that a growing number of people express their abhorrence of the breaches of ethical conduct by national and local leaders and that a vast majority of the populace believe that ethics play a critical role in leadership.

John Gardner (1990) thoughtfully makes the connection between shared values and a moral commitment to do the right thing. He reflects:

> In any functioning society everything—leadership and everything else—takes place within a set of shared beliefs concerning the standards of acceptable behavior that must govern individual members. One of the tasks of leadership—at all levels—is to revitalize those shared beliefs and values, and to draw on them as sources of motivation for the exertions required of the group. Leaders can help to keep the values fresh. They can combat the hypocrisy that proclaims values at the same time that it violates them. They can help us understand our history and our present dilemmas. They have a role in creating the state of mind that is the society. Leaders must conceive and articulate goals in ways that lift people out of their petty preoccupations and unite them toward higher ends. (p. 191)

Gardner implies that leadership "toward higher ends" is ethical in nature and includes positive, constructive ends rather than results or outcomes that are destructive, harmful, or immoral.

To underscore the importance of the relationship between leadership and ethics, we join with those scholars who propose that ethics is the central core of leadership. Without a commitment to doing the right thing or a sound code of ethical standards, leadership cannot emerge. Although some argue that the phrase "ethical leadership" is redundant because leadership cannot be experienced without an element of ethics, we feel that leadership that lacks ethical behavior and actions is anything but leadership. Consider the example of Adolf Hitler. Indeed, right now you may be thinking that Hitler was a leader but you are averse to what he was leading, and some leadership theorists would agree with you. We share the views of other scholars, however, that Hitler's actions were not aligned with our notions of leadership. They were acts of dictatorship (Burns, 1978).

Burns (1978) elevates the importance of values and ethics in the leadership process through his theory of transforming leadership. He notes that "the ultimate test of moral leadership is its capacity to transcend the claims of multiplicity of everyday wants and needs and expectations, to respond to the higher levels of moral development, and to relate leadership behavior—its roles, choices, style, commitments—to a set of reasoned, relatively explicit, conscious values" (p. 46). Aligned with Burns's bold thinking to cast leadership in a moral foundation is the recent shift in societal views, from leadership as values-neutral to leadership as values-driven (Beck & Murphy, 1994; Bok, 1982, 1990; Gandossy & Effron, 2004; Kouzes & Posner, 2002; Northouse, 2004; Piper, Gentile, & Parks, 1993). Moral or ethical leadership is driven by knowing what is virtuous and what is good.

Leading by Example

As an exercise, a leader and a participant must ponder soul-searching questions such as, What do I stand for? How far am I willing to go to advance the common good or to do the right thing? Based on their research on leaders, Kouzes and Posner (1987) propose five practices of exemplary leadership. One of these practices is "Modeling the Way" or practicing what one preaches. Leaders "show others by their own example that they live by the values that they profess" (p. 187). What one stands for "provides a prism through which all behavior is ultimately viewed" (p. 192).

Leading by example is a powerful way to influence the values and ethics of an organization. This means aligning your own values with the worthy values of the organization. Exemplary leadership includes a congruency between values and actions. The aphorism attributed to Ralph Waldo Emerson—"What you do speaks so loudly that I cannot hear what you say"—implies an even greater emphasis on the importance of values being congruent with actions. Nobel Peace Prize recipient Jimmy Carter is the first contemporary president said to have pursued higher goals after the presidency. Indeed, his work in diplomacy and in community service such as Habitat for Humanity attests to the congruence between his values and his actions. It is one thing to profess values and quite another to act on them.

Terry (1993) provides a cautionary note that action without authenticity erodes what can be considered ethical or moral leadership. Terry defines authenticity as "genuineness and a refusal to engage in self deception" (p. 128). Being true to oneself as a leader is a prerequisite for ethical and moral leadership.

The task of leading by example is not an easy one. Most, if not all, leaders begin with the goal of wanting to do the right thing. Some leaders get derailed by peer pressure or the temptation to trade leading for the common good with leading for personal gain or the uncommon good. What sustains ethical and moral leadership is a stubborn commitment to high standards, which include honesty and trustworthiness, authenticity, organizational values, and doing the right thing. It takes courage and chutzpah to stand among your peers and advocate a decision that is right yet unpopular. Imagine the tremendous courage of a fraternity chapter member or ROTC junior officer who says, "No, I do not think we should make our pledges drink until they pass out and then drop them off naked in the woods. It is not only dangerous but it is not how I want to bring them into our brotherhood. I won't be a part of it, and I hope you will not either. I will help plan activities that are fun and more worthwhile, but we cannot do this." Or the courage of a student who steps in and stops his peers from flipping over a car during a campus riot.

"To handle ethical dilemmas, the single most important quality to remember is to be honest with yourself and others. Tell the parties involved honestly and openly how you feel about the particular issue. Help them understand delicately your position, but stand strong in the dilemma. One other important aspect is listening and not jumping to conclusions."—Andrea Jean Grate, from Alfred University, was a director of student orientation.

Although it appears that we are stating the obvious by stressing the importance of leading by example and with integrity, there are, regrettably, numerous accounts of local and national leaders who have been caught embezzling, putting humans at risk for the sake of profit, and hiding the truth. Richard M. Nixon began his presidency with good intentions and then succumbed to political corruption. Leading with integrity is not a neat and tidy process, yet it probably is the driving force that allows leaders to continue in their capacities.

Relational Leadership Is about Process

Process refers to how the group goes about being a group, remaining a group, and accomplishing a group's purposes. It refers to the recruitment and involvement of members, how the group makes decisions, and how the group handles the tasks related to its mission and vision. Every group has a process, and every process can be described. Processes must be intentional and not incidental. The process component of the Relational Leadership Model means that individuals interact with others and that leaders and other participants work together to accomplish change. The process creates energy, synergy, and momentum.

When asked how her view of the universe as orderly in its chaotic state has influenced her work with organizations, Wheatley (1992) observed, "The time I formerly spent on detailed planning and analysis I now use to look at the structures that might facilitate relationships. I have come to expect that something useful occurs if I link up people, units, or tasks, even though I cannot determine precise outcomes" (p. 43–44). When groups design and implement ethical, inclusive, empowering processes that further a shared purpose, they can trust the processes to take them through difficult times, resolve ambiguous tasks, and be assured that together they will be better than they might be individually.

Too often, processes devalue the people involved by being highly controlled, valuing winning at all costs, excluding or shutting out those who have an interest in change, or expecting everyone to think and act alike. Attending to the process means being thoughtful and conscious of how the group is going about its business, so participants might say, "Wait a minute. If we do it this way, we'll be ignoring the needs of an important group of students and that is not our intent." Wheatley (2003) believes that we live in a process world. She states that "we would do better to attend more carefully to the process by which we create our plans and intentions. We need to see these plans, standards, organization charts not as objects that we complete, but as processes that enable a group to keep clarifying its intent and strengthening its connections to new people and new information" (p. 516).

Several key processes are essential to relational leadership. These processes include collaboration, reflection, feedback, civil confrontation, community building, and a level of profound understanding called *meaning making*. We will discuss several of these here and in subsequent chapters. Being process-oriented means that participants and the group as a whole are conscious of their process. They are reflective, challenging, collaborative, and caring. Being process-oriented means being aware of the dynamics among people in groups. Many groups jump right into the task or goal and lose a focus on the process. When participants focus on the process of group life or community life, they are forced to ask, Why do we do things this way? How could we be more effective? Participants ensure that the groups keeps working and learning together.

Cooperation and Collaboration

Competition seems embedded in many of our American structures. The adversarial legal system, sports teams, the game of poker, and the competitive free market economy all illustrate the way competition permeates our shared life. It is hard to imagine a different paradigm. Even while avoiding trying to beat others and not needing to always be number one, many people feel a strong need to compete with themselves. Perhaps they need to better that last exam grade or beat their last video game score.

In the early 1980s, researchers at the University of Minnesota reviewed 122 studies conducted over a fifty-year period on the role of competitive, cooperative, or individual goal orientations in achievement. Researchers concluded that "cooperation is superior to competition in promoting achievement and productivity" (Johnson, Maruyama, Johnson, Nelson, & Skon, 1981, p. 56). They further distinguished the strong benefits of cooperation (not competition) in the internal functioning of the group from the incentives when competing with other external groups (Johnson et al.). Working cooperatively with other participants is a desirable process.

Studies consistently show that members of various kinds of groups prefer positional leaders and colleagues who establish cooperative or collaborative relationships with them instead of competitive relationships (Kanter, 1989; Spence, 1983; Tjosvold & Tjosvold, 1991). Even a group member who enjoys competition in athletics is not likely to enjoy working in a setting such as a sports team, committee, study group, or job site in which others are competitive and try to beat each other or use competitive practices like withholding information or degrading others' contributions. Indeed, "the simplest way to understand why competition generally does not promote excellence is to realize that trying to do well and trying to beat others are two different things" (Kohn, 1992, p. 55). A person's best work is done under conditions of support and cooperation, not under fear, anxiety, or coercion.

The concepts of cooperation and collaboration are different.

> Collaboration is more than simply sharing knowledge and information (communication) and more than a relationship that helps each party achieve its own goals (cooperation and coordination). The purpose of collaboration is to create a shared vision and joint strategies to address concerns that go beyond the purview of any particular party. (Chrislip & Larson, 1994, p. 5)

Wood and Gray (1991) assert that "collaboration occurs when a group of autonomous stakeholders of a problem engage in an interactive process, using shared rules, norms, and structures, to act or decide on issues related to that domain" (p. 146). For example, Microsoft and Intel collaborated on developing wireless applications for PDAs and smart phones. These companies had a shared vision that was achieved by working together rather than in competition with each other. Former presidents George H. W. Bush and Bill Clinton, who were once in fierce political competition with one another, worked collaboratively on natural disaster relief projects in the face of the Southeast Asian tsunami in 2004 and Hurricane Katrina in 2005.

Both cooperation and collaboration are helpful processes: cooperation helps the other person or group achieve their own goals, whereas collaboration joins with another person or group in setting and accomplishing mutual, shared goals. The "collaborative premise" is a belief that "if you bring the appropriate people together in constructive ways with good information, they will create authentic visions and strategies for addressing the shared concerns of the organization or community" (Chrislip & Larson, p. 14). It would be cooperation for the Habitat for Humanity group to send their membership recruitment flyer out with the Food Cooperative flyer to save postage or for them to attend another group's event. It would be collaboration for those two groups and several others with a common environmental purpose to design a new flyer to attract new members to these shared causes or to work collaboratively together to plan a larger event.

"Part of being a leader is being a participant as well because by being a leader, you need to lead by example. Taking part in whatever you are leading will show that you are proud and enthusiastic to be involved with your particular group. Other members will also respect the fact that you are not only a leader, but that you are humble enough to participate like everyone else."—Betsy Dedels is a member of Phi Beta Kappa and team captain of intramural volleyball. She majors in sociology at the University of Kentucky.

For the group to be effective, all members must be prepared to do their part.

Music provides a good metaphor for this kind of teamwork. Musicians must be individually skilled and committed, yet know that they are part of a collective—a team. Further, imagine a performance of jazz music with improvisational dance. Both dancers and musicians find wonderful rhythms and sounds, simultaneously interpreted, shaping each other's work. The collaboration, respect, and commitment to their common purposes as dancers and musicians are obvious. Yet those artists did not just walk into a studio and create movement. The dancers knew their bodies and the musicians knew their instruments. They knew how and why and when to react. Their self-awareness of their own strengths, limits, talents, and abilities created the collaboration in their joint effort. In a parallel manner, think of a terrific class project in which individuals volunteer their knowledge and skills ("I can do the Power-Point presentation" or "I can call those businesses for donations"), and the division of labor starts to shape a strong project. Knowing yourself well and seeking to know the members of the group creates a group atmosphere conducive to collaboration.

Meaning Making

Leadership requires a process of truly understanding (that is, making meaning) throughout the shared experience of the group. Meaning has both cognitive (ideas and thoughts) and emotional (feelings) components, which "allows a person to know (in the sense of understand) some world version (a representation of the way things are and the way they ought to be) and that places the person in relation to this world view" (Drath & Palus, 1994, p. 4). Part of this meaning making involves the recognition that in our rapidly changing world, we are continually challenged to see that data become information, information becomes translated into knowledge, knowledge influences understanding, understanding translates into wisdom, and wisdom becomes meaningful thought and action. Imagine this flow as

DATA → INFORMATION → KNOWLEDGE →
UNDERSTANDING → WISDOM →
THOUGHT AND ACTION

Meaning making is "the process of arranging our understanding of experience so that we can know what has happened and what is happening, and so that we can predict what will happen; it is constructing knowledge of ourselves and the world" (Drath & Palus, 1994, p. 2). Drath and Palus make it clear that two understandings of the word *meaning* guide our thinking about meaning and leadership. One use is when symbols, like words, stand for something. This process of *naming* and *interpreting* helps clarify meaning and is essential for the perspectives needed in reframing and seeing multiple realities. For example, one person might call a particular action lawlessness, and another might call it civil disobedience. What one person might call destructive partying, another might see as group bonding and celebration. Coming to agreement on the interpretations of symbolic words and events helps a group to make meaning. Senge (1990) refers to these as "mental models."

The second use of the word *meaning* involves "people's values and relationships and commitments" (Drath & Palus, 1994, p. 7). People want to matter and to lead lives of meaning. When something is of value, one can make a commitment, find personal purpose, and risk personal involvement—it matters, it has meaning. In contrast, if something is meaningless or of no value, then it does not engage emotion and build commitment. However, we should be careful not to judge too quickly. Sometimes, important matters may seem to have no value. For example, a group of students expressing concern about getting to their cars in remote parking lots after late-night classes deserves a careful hearing. Those listening may be student government officers who live in nearby residence halls or campus administrators who have parking spaces near their buildings. The relational empathy skill of trying to see things from the perspective of another will validate that meaning.

Understanding how we make meaning helps a group frame and reframe the issues and problems they are seeking to resolve. The framing process involves naming the problem and identifying the nature of interventions or solutions that might be helpful. If a problem is framed as, "The administration won't provide money for additional safety lighting," it leads to a set of discussions and strategies focused on changing the administration. Reframing means finding a new interpretation of the problem that might create a new view that helps a group be more productive (Bryson & Crosby, 1992). Reframing this same problem might bring a new awareness of coalitions, shareholders, and stakeholders if it were readdressed as, "How can we unite the talent of our campus to address the problem of a dramatic rise in crimes against women?"

Reflection and Contemplation

Vaill (1989) proposes that the rapid pace of change and the need to make meaning from ambiguous material requires individuals and groups to practice reflection. Reflection is the process of pausing, stepping back from the action, and asking, What is happening? Why is this happening? What does this mean? What does this mean for me? What can I learn from this? Lao Tzu (Heider, 1985) encourages time for reflection:

> Endless drama in a group clouds consciousness. Too much noise overwhelms the senses. Continual input obscures genuine insight. Do not substitute sensationalism for learning. Allow regular time for silent reflection. Turn inward

and digest what has happened. Let the senses rest and grow still. Teach people to let go of their superficial mental chatter and obsessions. Teach people to pay attention to the whole body's reaction to a situation. When group members have time to reflect, they can see more clearly what is essential in themselves and others. (p. 23)

Smith, MacGregor, Matthews, and Gabelnick (2004) believe that "reflective thinking should be metacognitive" (p. 125). Metacognition is "thinking about one's thinking—now considered essential for effective learning and problem solving" (p. 126). Reflection can be accomplished when a group intentionally discusses its process. If groups discuss their process at all, they usually reflect only on their failures. They try to find out what went wrong and how to avoid those errors again. To be true learning organizations, groups also need to reflect on their successes and bring to every participant's awareness a common understanding of answers to such questions as, Why did this go so well? What did we do together that made this happen? How can we make sure to work this well together again? Horwood (1989) observes that "Reflection is hard mental work. The word itself means 'bending back.' . . . The mental work of reflection includes deliberation . . . rumination . . . pondering . . . and musing" (p. 5). Reflection is a key process in becoming a learning community.

In a study of successful leaders, Bennis (1989) observed that these effective leaders encouraged "reflective backtalk" (p. 194). They knew the importance of truth telling and encouraged their colleagues to reflect honestly what they think they saw or heard. "Reflection is vital—at every level, in every organization ... all [leaders] should practice the new three Rs: retreat, renewal, and return" (p. 186). One form of group reflection is when the group processes (discusses) a shared experience. As a difficult meeting winds down, any participant (or perhaps the group's adviser) might say, "Let's take time now at the end of this meeting to process what we liked about how we handled the big decision tonight and what we think we should do differently next time." Reflection is also useful for keeping a group on track. A group might intentionally review its goals and mission in the middle of the year and discuss how their activities are supporting that mission or whether they should be redirected. Reflection is an essential component of a process to keep individuals and the whole group focused and intentional.

Contemplation is a form of reflection that allows us to think deeply about the events around us, our feelings, and our emotions. Chickering, Dalton, and Stamm (2006) describe contemplation as "the cerebral metabolic process for meaning making. The food that we chew and swallow, that then enters our stomach, only nourishes us, only becomes part of our bloodstream, muscles, nerves, and body chemistry when it is metabolized" (p. 143). The experiences of life operate in a similar way. In the absence of reflection and contemplation, the knowledge that we acquire and the experiences that we go through can "end up like the residue from food we don't metabolize" (p. 143). Reflective practices allow us to think about what is occurring around us and to us and then to make meaning from those experiences.

What Would This Look Like?

You will acquire many leadership skills over time. It is easy to confuse some management tools—like running meetings or planning agendas—with real leadership. Using the principles of relational leadership, you can reframe typical skills like agenda planning so that they are more effective. The goals of the agenda for your group meeting will not be just to get through the topics to be presented or decided in the quickest time but will involve the most people, empower voices that might have been excluded before, make sure no one is railroaded and that fair decisions are made, involve others in building an agenda, and use collaborative practices.

Remember the times you have been to a meeting whose leader made all the announcements. A small group of two or three in-group members seemed to run the whole show, and you never said a word. We have all had that experience. You felt marginalized and might have wondered why you even bothered to attend. Think of a meeting in which people disagreed hotly and then someone quickly moved to vote on an issue. A vote was taken with the resulting majority winning and a dissatisfied minority losing or feeling railroaded.

Imagine the differences in a meeting whose positional leader or convener says, "It is our custom to make sure everyone is involved and heard before we try to resolve issues. The executive committee has asked three of you to present the key issues on the first agenda item; we will then break into small groups for fifteen minutes to see what questions and issues emerge before we proceed and see what we want to do at that point. In your discussion, try to identify the principles that will be important for us to consider in the decision we eventually make." Even if you do not agree with this approach, you would feel more comfortable suggesting a different model because the tone of the meeting is one of involvement and participation.

Chapter Summary

Conditions in our rapidly changing world require that each of us become effective members of our groups and communities in order to work with others toward needed change and for common purpose. The way we relate to each other matters and is symbolic of our social responsibility. Taking the time needed to build a sense of community in a group acknowledges that relationships are central to effective leadership. Relational leadership is purposeful, inclusive, empowering, ethical, and about process. Attention to those practices builds a strong organization with committed participants who know they matter.

Additional Readings

Bennis, W. G., & Thomas, R. J. (2002). *Geeks and geezers: How era, values, and defining moments shape leaders.* Boston: Harvard Business School Press.

Chrislip, D. D., & Larson, C. E. (1994). *Collaborative leadership: How citizens and civic leaders can make a difference.* San Francisco: Jossey-Bass.

Drath, W. H., & Palus, C. J. (1994). *Making common sense: Leadership as meaning-making in a community of practice.* Greensboro, NC: Center for Creative Leadership.

Gandossy, R., & Effron, M. (2004). *Leading the way: Three truths from the top companies for leaders.* Hoboken, NJ; Wiley.

Kouzes, J. M., & Posner, B. Z. (2002). *The leadership challenge* (3rd ed.). San Francisco: Jossey-Bass.

Attitude, Goal Setting, and Life Management

by Lydia E. Anderson
and Sandra B. Bolt

The future belongs to those who believe in the beauty of their dreams.

Eleanor Roosevelt (1884–1962)

Objectives

- Define *professionalism*
- Define and describe *personality* and *attitude* and their influence in the workplace
- Identify individual personality traits and *values*
- Identify the influences of *self-efficacy*
- Identify and develop a strategy to deal with past negative experiences
- Define *locus of control*
- Identify primary and secondary *learning styles*
- Describe the importance of *goal setting*
- Identify the impact setting goals and objectives have on a life plan
- Set realistic goals
- Define goal-setting techniques
- Create *short-term* and *long-term goals*
- Describe the importance of setting *priorities*

How-Do-You-Rate

	Are you self-centered?	Yes	No
1.	Do you rarely use the word "I" in conversations?	❑	❑
2.	When in line with coworkers, do you let coworkers go ahead of you?	❑	❑
3.	Do you keep personal work accomplishments private?	❑	❑
4.	Do you rarely interrupt conversations?	❑	❑
5.	Do you celebrate special events (e.g., birthdays, holidays) with your coworkers by sending them a card, a note, or small gift?	❑	❑

If you answered "yes" to two or more of these questions, well done. Your actions are more focused on the needs of others and you are most likely not self-centered.

All About You

Congratulations! You are about to embark on a self-discovery to identify how to become and remain productive and successful in the workplace. The first step in this self-discovery is to perform a simple exercise. Look in a mirror and write the first three words that immediately come to mind.

1. _____.

2. _____.

3. _____.

These three words are your mirror words. **Mirror words** describe the foundation of how you view yourself, how you view others, and how you will most likely perform in the workplace.

This text is all about professionalism in the workplace. The goal of both your instructor and the authors is to not only help you secure the job of your dreams, but more importantly to keep that great job and advance your career based upon healthy, quality, and productive work habits that benefit you, your coworkers, and your organization. **Professionalism** is defined as workplace behaviors that result in positive business relationships. This text provides you tools to help you experience a more fulfilling and productive career. The secret to healthy relationships at work is to first understand you. Once you understand your personal needs, motivators, and irritants, it becomes easier to understand and successfully work with others. This is why the first part of this chapter focuses on your personality, your values, and your self-concept.

An individual's personality and attitude dictate how he or she responds to conflict, crisis, and other typical workplace situations. Each of these typical workplace situations involves working with and through people. Understanding your own personality and attitude makes it much easier to understand your reactions to others' personalities and attitudes.

The workplace is comprised of people. **Human relations** are the interactions that occur with and through people. These interactions create relationships. Therefore, you theoretically have relationships with everyone you come into contact with at work. For an organization to be profitable, its employees must be productive. It is difficult to be productive if you cannot work with your colleagues, bosses, vendors, and/or customers. Workplace productivity is a result of positive workplace interactions and relationships.

Personality is a result of influences, and there are many outside influences that affect workplace relationships. These influences may include immediate family, friends, extended family, religious affiliation, and even society as a whole. This means that your experiences and influences outside of work affect your workplace behavior. It also means that experiences and influences at work affect your personal life. Therefore, to understand workplace relationships, you must first understand yourself.

Personality and Values

Behavior is a reflection of personality. **Personality** is a stable set of traits that assist in explaining and predicting an individual's behavior. Personality traits can be positive, such as being caring, considerate, organized, enthusiastic, or reliable. However, personality traits can also be negative, such as being rude, unfocused, lazy, or immature. For example, if your personality typically reflects being organized at work and suddenly you become disorganized, others may believe something is wrong because your disorganized behavior is not in sync with your typical stable set of organized traits. An individual's personality is shaped by many variables, including past experience, family, friends, religion, and societal influences. Perhaps a family member was incredibly organized and passed this trait on to you. Maybe someone in your sphere of influence was incredibly unorganized, which influenced you to be very organized. These experiences (positive or not) shape your values. **Values** are things that are important to you as an individual based upon your personal experiences and influences. These influences include religion, family, and societal issues such as sexual preference, political affiliation, and materialism. Note that you may have good or bad values. You may value achievement, family, money, security, or freedom. For example, one individual may not value money because he or she has been told that "money is the root of all evil." Contrast this with an individual who values money because he or she has been taught that money is a valuable resource used to ensure a safe, secure future. Since values are things that are important to you, they will directly affect your personality. If you have been taught that money is a valuable resource, you may be very careful in your spending. Your personality trait will be that of a diligent, hardworking person who spends cautiously.

Here is an example of how one's past experience shapes one's values. Cory's parents were both college graduates with successful careers. Cory worked hard to secure a new job. Cory continues to go to college and achieve success at work because the influences from the past impact Cory's values and beliefs in the ability to perform successfully at work. However, many of Cory's friends are

Talk It Out

What cartoon character
best reflects you?

not attending college, and many have a hard time securing and/or maintaining employment. For this reason, Cory gets no support from these friends regarding earning a degree and securing employment.

As explained in the example of Cory's values, those values are affecting both career and life choices. These are positive choices for Cory, but negative choices for some of Cory's friends.

Attitude

An **attitude** is a strong belief toward people, things, and situations. For example, you either care or do not care how your classmates feel about you. Your past success and failures affect your attitude. Your attitude is related to your values and personality. Using the previous money example, if you value money, then your attitude will be positive toward work, because you value what you get in return for your work effort—a paycheck. Attitude affects performance. An individual's performance significantly influences a group's performance. A group's performance, in turn, impacts an organization's performance. Think about a barrel of juicy red apples. Place one bad apple in the barrel of good apples, and, over time, the entire barrel will be spoiled. That is why it is so important to evaluate your personal influences. The barrel reflects your personal goals and your workplace behavior. Your attitude affects not only your performance, but also the performance of those with whom you come in contact.

Does this mean you avoid anyone you believe is a bad influence? Not necessarily. You cannot avoid certain individuals, such as relatives and coworkers. However, you should be aware of the impact individuals have on your life. If certain individuals have a negative influence, avoid or limit your exposure to the negative influence (bad apple). If you continue to expose yourself to negative influences, you can lose sight of your goals, which may result in a poor attitude and poor performance.

Self-Efficacy and Its Influences

Let us review your "mirror words" from the beginning of this chapter. What did you see? Are your words positive, or negative? Whatever you are feeling is a result of your **self-concept.** Self-concept is how you view yourself. Thinking you are intelligent or believing you are attractive are examples of self-concept. **Self-image** is your belief of how others view you. If your self-concept is positive and strong, you will reflect confidence and not worry about how others view you and your actions. If you are insecure, you will rely heavily on what others think of you. While it is important to show concern for what others think of you, it is more important to have a positive self-concept. Note that there is a difference between being conceited and self-confident. Behaving in a conceited manner means you have too high an opinion of yourself as compared to others. People are drawn to individuals who are humble, display a good attitude, are confident, and are consistently positive. If you believe in yourself, a positive self-image will follow without effort. It is easy to see the tremendous impact both personality and attitude have in the development of your self-concept and self-image. One final factor that influences self-concept and performance is that of self-efficacy. **Self-efficacy** is your belief in your ability to perform a task. For example, if you are confident in your math abilities, you will most likely score high on a math exam because you believe you are strong in that subject. However, if you are required to take a math placement exam for a job and you are not confident in your math abilities, you will most likely not perform well. The way you feel about yourself and your environment is reflected in how you treat others. This is called **projection.** If you have a positive self-concept, this will be projected in a positive manner toward others.

Envision a hand mirror. The handle of the mirror (the foundation) is your personality. The frame of the mirror is your personal values. The mirror itself is your attitude, which is reflected for you and the world to see. The way you view yourself is your self-concept; the way you believe others see you is your self-image.

Exercise 3-1   All About You

Describe yourself. Include your personality traits, personal values and attitude toward achieving career success.

_____

_____

_____

Dealing with Negative "Baggage"

Many of us have experienced a person who appears to have a "chip on his or her shoulder" that negatively influences his or her behavior. This is reflected in the individual's personality. More often than not, this "chip" is a reflection of a painful past experience. What many do not realize is that our negative past experiences sometimes turn into personal baggage that creates barriers to career success. Examples of negative past experiences may include traumatic issues such as an unplanned pregnancy or a criminal offense. Other times, the negative experience involved a poor choice or a failure at something that had great meaning. These experiences are the ones that most heavily impact one's personality, values, and self-esteem. In turn, this will affect your attitude at the workplace, which will eventually affect your performance. Consider the following example concerning Cory. In high school, Cory made a poor choice and got in minor trouble with the law. Cory paid the dues, yet is still embarrassed and sometimes still feels unworthy of a successful future. Cory is trying to climb the mountain of success carrying a hundred-pound suitcase. The suitcase is filled with the thoughts of previous poor choices and embarrassment. From others' perspective, Cory does not need to carry this unnecessary baggage. In fact, because of Cory's motivation to complete college, most friends and acquaintances are unaware of Cory's past mistake. Cory's current self-efficacy leads Cory to believe success cannot be attained. Cory needs to learn from and forgive the past mistake and move forward. As self-image improves, Cory's belief in the ability to succeed will increase.

If you are one of these individuals who have had a negative experience that is hindering your ability to succeed, recognize the impact your past has on your future. Although you cannot change yesterday, you can most certainly improve your today and your future. Begin taking these steps toward a more productive future:

1. *Confront your past.* Whatever skeleton is in your past, admit that the event occurred. Do not try to hide or deny that it happened. There is no need to share the episode with everyone, but it may help to confidentially share the experience with one individual (close friend, family member, religious leader, or trained professional) who had no involvement with the negative experience. Self-talk is the first step toward healing. Verbally talk through your feelings, reminding yourself of your positive assets.

2. *Practice forgiveness.* Past negative experiences create hurt. A process in healing is to forgive whoever hurt you. This does not justify what was done as acceptable. The act of forgiveness does, however, reconcile in your heart that you are dealing with the experience and are beginning to heal. Identify who needs forgiveness. Maybe it is a family member, perhaps it is a friend or neighbor, or maybe it is you. Your act of forgiveness may involve a conversation with someone, or it may just involve a conversation with yourself. Practice forgiveness. In doing so, you will begin to feel a huge burden being lifted.

3. *Move forward.* Let go of guilt and/or embarrassment. Once you have begun dealing with your past, move forward. Do not keep dwelling on the past and using it as an excuse or barrier toward achieving your goals. If you are caught in this step, physically write the experience down on a piece of paper and the words "I forgive Joe" (replace the name with the individual who harmed you). Then take the paper and destroy it. This physical act puts you in control and allows you to visualize the negative experience being diminished. As you become more confident in yourself, your negative experience becomes enveloped with the rest of your past and frees you to create a positive future.

This sometimes painful process is necessary if your goal is to become the best individual you can be. It is not something that happens overnight. As mentioned previously, some individuals may need professional assistance to help them through the process. There is no shame in seeking help. In fact, there is great freedom when you have finally let go of the "baggage" and are able to climb to the top of the mountain unencumbered.

Exercise 3-2   Letting Go

How should Cory deal with the negative baggage?

_____

_____

_____

Locus of Control

The reality is that you will not always be surrounded by positive influences and you cannot control everything that happens in your life. Your attitude is affected by who you believe has control over situations that occur in your life, both personally and professionally. The **locus of control** identifies who you believe controls your future. An individual with an *internal* locus of control believes that he or she controls his or her own future. An individual with an *external* locus of control believes that others control his or her future.

Extremes on either end of the locus of control are not healthy. Realize that individual effort and a belief in the ability to perform well translate to individual success. However, external factors also influence your ability to achieve personal goals. Take responsibility for your actions and try your best. You cannot totally control the environment and future. Power, politics, and other factors discussed later in the text play an important part in the attainment of goals.

Learning Styles

Another element of personality is one's **learning style.** Learning styles define the method of how you best take in information and/or learn new ideas. There are three primary learning styles: visual, auditory, and tactile/kinesthetic.

To determine what your dominant learning style is, perform this simple exercise. Imagine you are lost and need directions. Do you:

a. want to see a map,
b. want someone to tell you the directions, or
c. need to draw or write down the directions yourself?

If you prefer answer *a,* you are a visual learner. You prefer learning by seeing. If you selected *b,* you are an auditory learner. You learn best by hearing. If you selected *c,* you are a tactile/kinesthetic learner, which means you learn best by feeling, touching, or holding. No one learning style is better than the other. However, it is important to recognize your primary and secondary learning styles so that you can get the most out of your world (in and out of the classroom or on the job). As a visual learner, you may digest material best by reading and researching. Auditory learners pay close attention to course lectures and class discussions. Tactile/kinesthetic learners will learn best by performing application exercises and physically writing course notes. Recognize what works best for you and implement that method to maximize your learning experience. Also recognize that not everyone learns the same way you do and not all information is presented in your preferred method. With that recognition, you can become a better classmate, team member, coworker, and boss.

Your Personal Handbook

The main idea of this discussion is that personality and attitude affect performance both personally and professionally. If you can honestly say that you have no concerns regarding personal confidence, attitude, and external influences (friends and family), congratulations. You have just crossed the first big hurdle toward workplace success. If you are like the majority of the population and can identify opportunities for improvement with either internal or external influences, a bigger congratulation is extended to you. Identifying areas for improvement is by far one of the most difficult hurdles to jump but certainly the most rewarding.

This book is designed as a personal handbook that leads you on an exciting journey toward creating both personal and career plans. On this journey you will also develop a respect and understanding of basic personal financial management and the influence finances have on many areas of your life. Self-management skills including time, stress, and organization will be addressed, as well as professional etiquette and dress. Workplace politics, their implications on performance, and how to successfully use these politics in your favor will be discussed, as will your rights as an employee. These newfound workplace skills will improve your ability to lead, motivate, and successfully work with others in a team setting. Finally, you will learn how to handle conflict and work with difficult coworkers.

As we move through key concepts in this text, begin developing a positive attitude and believe in yourself and your abilities. Equally important is that you learn from your past. Little by little, you will make lifestyle changes that will make you a better individual, which will make you an even better employee. It all translates to success at work and success in life.

The Importance of Personal Goal Setting

Everyone has dreams. These dreams may be for a college degree, a better life for loved ones, financial security, or the acquisition of material items such as a new car or home. Goal setting is the first step toward turning a dream into a reality. This important process provides focus and identifies specific steps that need to be accomplished. It is also a common practice used by successful individuals and organizations. A **goal** is a target. Think of a goal as a reward at the top of a ladder. Goals typically come in two forms: short-term goals and long-term goals. To reach a long-term goal, you need to progress up each step of the ladder. Each step contributes to the achievement of a goal and supports your personal values. More difficult goals typically take longer to achieve. Goals provide focus; increase self-concept; and help overcome procrastination, fear, and failure.

Influences of Goals

When you set and focus on goals, career plans become more clear and meaningful. They motivate you to continue working to improve yourself and help you achieve, not just hope for, what you want in life.

Consider Cory's goals. At twenty-two years of age, Cory had only a high-school education. After working as a service clerk since graduating from high school, Cory decided to go to college to become a Certified Public Accountant (CPA). Cory's long-term goal is to finish college in five years. Self-supporting and having to work, Cory set a realistic goal to obtain an associate degree in accounting within three years. After achieving that goal, Cory found a good job, has a good income, and has more self-confidence. Still committed to becoming a CPA, Cory needs to earn a bachelor's degree and has set a goal to do that within two years. This is motivating Cory to perform well.

In Cory's example, as one goal was reached, Cory became more motivated and self-confident enough to set a higher goal. Achieving goals results in continually striving for improvement.

Goals can and should be set in all major areas of your life, including personal, career, financial, educational, and physical. Goals help maintain a positive outlook. They also contribute to creating a more positive perception of you and will result in improved human relations with others.

Talk It Out

Discuss one goal that can be set for this class.

How to Set Goals

As explained earlier, achieving short- and long-term goals is like climbing a ladder. Imagine that there is a major prize (what you value most) at the top of the ladder. The prize can be considered your long-term goal, and each step on the ladder is a progressive short-term goal that helps you reach the major prize.

Set short-term and long-term goals and put them in writing. **Long-term goals** are goals that will take longer than a year to accomplish, with a realistic window of up to ten years.

To set a goal, first identify what you want to accomplish in your life. Write down everything you can think of, including personal, career, and educational dreams. Next, review the list and choose which items you most value. In reviewing your list, ask yourself where you want to be in one year, five years, and ten years. The items you identified are your long-term goals. Keep each goal realistic and something you truly want. Each goal should be challenging enough that you will work toward it but it should also be attainable. There should be a reason to reach each goal. Identify why each goal is important to you. This is a key step toward setting yourself up for success. Identify both opportunities and potential barriers toward reaching these goals. Remember Cory's goal to be a CPA? Cory believes becoming a CPA represents success. It is important to Cory, and it is a realistic goal that can be reached.

Exercise 3-3   Long-Term Career Goal

Write your long-term career goal.

_____

_____

_____

Short-term goals are goals that can be reached within a year's time. Short-term goals are commonly set to help reach long-term goals. Businesses often refer to short-term goals as **objectives,** because they are short-term, measurable, and have specific time lines. Short-term goals can be achieved in one day, a week, a month, or even several months. As short-term goals are met, long-term goals should be updated.

Just like long-term goals, short-term goals (objectives) must be realistic, achievable, and important to you. They need to be measurable so you know when you have actually reached them.

An additional long-term goal for Cory is to buy a car one year after graduation. Cory has set several short-term goals, one being to save a specific amount of money each month. To do this, Cory needs to work a certain number of hours each week. Cory also needs to be specific about the type of car, whether to buy used or new, and whether he needs to take out a loan. The answers to these questions will determine if the time frame is realistic and how much Cory needs to save every month.

Exercise 3-4   Short-Term Goals

Using your long-term career goal from Exercise 3-3, identify at least three short term goals.

_____

_____

_____

A popular and easy goal-setting method is the SMART method. SMART is an acronym for "specific, measurable, achievable, relevant, and time-based." Clearly identify what exactly you want to accomplish and, if possible, make your goal quantifiable. This makes your goal specific. Also, make your goal measurable. Identify how you know when you have achieved your goal. Keep your goal achievable but not too easily attainable nor too far out of reach. A good achievable goal is challenging, yet attainable and realistic. Relevant personal goals have meaning to its owner. The goal should belong to you, and you should have (or have access to) the appropriate resources to accomplish the goal. Finally, **SMART goals** are time-based. Attaching a specific date or time period provides a time frame for achieving the goal. For example, instead of writing, "I will become a manager in the future," write, "I will become a manager with a top accounting firm by the beginning of the year 2018." After you have written a goal, give it the SMART test to increase its probability for success.

Exercise 3-5   SMART Goals

Rewrite the goals from Exercise 3-4 into SMART goals.

_____

_____

_____

After you have written your goals in a positive and detailed manner, there are a few additional aspects of goal setting to consider. These include owning and being in control of your goals.

Owning the goal ensures that the goal belongs to you. You should decide your goals, not your parents, spouse, significant other, friends, relatives, or anyone else who may have influence over you. For example, if Cory goes to college because it is a personal dream to be a CPA, that goal will be accomplished. However, if Cory becomes a CPA because it was Cory's parents' idea to be a CPA, this would not be Cory's goal and it would make it harder to accomplish this goal.

Control your goal by securing the right information necessary to accomplish it. Know what resources and constraints are involved, including how you will be able to use resources and/or get around constraints. If your goal is related to a specific career, identify what attaining it will require in regard to finances, education, and other matters. Clarify the time needed to reach these goals by writing them as short-term or long-term goals. Referring back to the concept of locus of control, remember that not every factor is within your control. Therefore, be flexible and maintain realistic control over your goal.

Creating a Life Plan

Identifying goals contribute to the creation of a **life plan.** A life plan is a written document that identifies goals in all areas of your life, including your career and personal life (social, spiritual, financial, and activities).

Consider the following life issues:

- *Education and career:* Degree attainment, advanced degrees, job titles, specific employers.
- *Social and spiritual:* Marriage, family, friends, religion.
- *Financial:* Home ownership, car ownership, investments.
- *Activities:* Travel, hobbies, life experiences.

Create goals for each of these major life areas and note that some of your goals may blend into two or more areas. Some younger students are uncertain of their career goals. Others may feel overwhelmed that they have a life goal but perhaps lack the necessary resources to accomplish a goal. Goals can change over time. Stay focused but flexible. What is important is that you establish goals that reflect your values.

Just as your personal life goals and career goals are important, education is an important key to achieving your life plan. Consider the degrees/certificates required, the time frame, the financial resources, and the support network you will require for educational success.

No one can ever take your knowledge away from you. Make college course choices based upon your desired educational goals. Choose courses that will benefit you, help you explore new concepts, and challenge you. To be successful in your career, it is important to enjoy what you do. Select a career that supports your short-term and long-term goals.

When planning your career consider:

- Why your selected career is important to you.
- What resources are needed to achieve your career goals.
- How you will know you have achieved career success.

People choose careers for different reasons, including earning power, status, intellect, values, and self-satisfaction. If there is a career center available at your college, take time to visit and explore the various resources it offers. There are also several personality and career interest tests you can take that will help you determine your potential career. One popular and useful career assessment is the Golden Personality Type Profiler. The Golden Profiler is a well-respected personality assessment that assists users in identifying behaviors that support specific careers. Additional career assessments are offered at many college career centers and online. These useful assessments help identify interests, abilities, and

Web Quiz

Discover your personality

Take the Golden Personality Type Profiler or search for another online personality test to take.

www.mystudentsuccesslab. com.

personality traits to determine which career will suit you best. Use all resources available and gather information to assist you in making the best career decision. Conduct Internet searches, interview people who are already working in your field of interest, perform an internship, volunteer, or job shadow in a field that interests you. Doing so will help clarify your goals and life plan. An additional discussion on career exploration is presented in a later chapter.

Consider the type of personal relationships you want in the future. Goals should reflect your choice of marriage, family, friends, and religion. Identify where you want to be financially. Many people dream of becoming a millionaire, but you need to be realistic. Think about what kind of house you want to live in and what type of car you want to drive. If a spouse and children are in your future, account for their financial needs, as well. Also identify what outside activities you enjoy, including hobbies and travel. The personal financial plan you create will be a part of achieving these goals. This will be discussed in more detail in the next chapter. Think about what results and rewards will come from achieving your goals.

Intrinsic rewards include such things as self-satisfaction and pride of accomplishment. These come from within you and are what you value in life. **Extrinsic rewards** include such things as money and praise. These rewards come from external sources. Intrinsic and extrinsic rewards are needed to achieve satisfaction in your future. Both are equally important and should be recognized. They motivate you and help you maintain a positive outlook when working toward goals.

Talk It Out

Share common rewards that are important to you. Identify these rewards as intrinsic or extrinsic.

Priorities

Priorities determine what needs to be done and in what order. Properly managing priorities is the key to reaching goals. Not only is it important in your personal life, but it will be necessary at work.

You may need to adjust priorities to reach your goals. Before priorities can be placed in order, determine what they are. Sometimes your first priority is not necessarily what is most important in life; it is just that a particular activity demands the most attention at a specific point in time. For example, if Cory has a young child, that child is one of the most important things in Cory's life. However, if Cory is attending college to become a CPA and needs an evening to study for a big exam, the priority will be to study for the exam. That does not mean the exam is more important than the child. However, passing the exam is a step toward a better future for Cory and the child.

Cory's decision is called a **trade-off.** A trade-off is giving up one thing to do something else. Another example involving Cory is the decision to purchase a car in one year; Cory needs to save a certain amount of money each month. In order to do this, Cory may have to give up going to the coffee shop each morning and instead make coffee at home in order to set aside enough money to meet the savings goal to purchase the car.

Life plans require flexibility. When working toward goals, be flexible. Times change, technology changes, and priorities may change, which influence your goals. Reevaluate goals at least once a year. You may need to update or revise your goals and/or time lines more frequently than once a year because a situation changed. If that is the case, be flexible and update the goals. Do not abandon your goals because the situation changed.

Talk It Out

Identify priorities and trade-offs for successfully completing this course.

Workplace Dos and Don'ts

Do realize the impact your personality has on overall workplace performance	*Don't* assume that everyone thinks and behaves like you
Do believe that you are a talented, capable human being. Project self-confidence	*Don't* become obsessed with how others view you. Be and do your best
Do let go of past baggage	*Don't* keep telling everyone about a past negative experience
Do set goals in writing	*Don't* set goals that are impossible to reach
Do set long-term and short-term goals	*Don't* give up on goals
Do make your goals attainable	*Don't* wait to create goals
Do have measurable goals	*Don't* create unrealistic goals
Do set priorities. Include trade-offs and flexibility when setting goals	*Don't* give up when working to reach your goals

Concept Review and Application

Summary of Key Concepts

- How you view yourself dictates how you treat others and what type of employee you will be
- Your views of yourself, your environment, and your past experiences comprise your personality, values, attitude, and self-efficacy
- Negative past experiences create unnecessary baggage that either delays or prevents you from reaching your goals. Acknowledge and begin dealing with these negative experiences

- There are three primary learning styles: visual, auditory, and tactile/kinesthetic (sight, sound, and touch). Individuals must recognize how they best learn and also be aware that others may or may not share their same learning style
- Goal setting is important in helping you keep focused. It will increase your self-concept and help you become more successful in all areas of your life
- As goals are reached, motivation and self-confidence will increase
- Goals need to be put into writing. They need to be realistic and measurable. Know who owns the goals and who controls the goals. A time frame is needed to know when you plan on reaching these goals
- Long-term goals are set to be achieved in five to ten years
- Short-term goals are achieved within a year's time and are needed to reach long-term goals
- When creating a life plan, consider all aspects of your life, including personal, career, and education
- Flexibility and properly managing priorities are needed to successfully achieve goals
- As you begin a new job, establish a relationship with a mentor

Key Terms

attitude	extrinsic rewards	goal
human relations	intrinsic rewards	learning style
life plan	locus of control	long-term goals
mirror words	objectives	personality
priorities	professionalism	projection
self-concept	self-efficacy	self-image
short-term goals	SMART goal	trade-off
values		

If You Were the Boss

1. How would you deal with an employee who displays poor self-efficacy?
2. How would recognizing different learning styles help you be a better boss?
3. Why does an employer need to set goals?
4. Why is it important that an employer ensure that employees set personal and career goals?

Web Links

http://www.humanmetrics.com/cgi-win/JTypes1.htm
http://www.colorquiz.com
http://personality-project.org/personality.html
http://www.ncrel.org/sdrs/areas/issues/students/learning/lr2locus.htm
http://www.mindtools.com/pages/article/newHTE_06.htm
http://www.topachievement.com/goalsetting.html
http://www.mygoals.com/helpGoalsettingTips.html
http://www.gems4friends.com/goals/index.html

S.M.A.R.T. Goals

S pecific
M easurable
A ttainable
R ealistic
T imely

Specific: The first component of any S.M.A.R.T. goal is its specificity. It should answer the following: Who What, Where, When, Which, and Why. Usually it is important that your goal is significant because those are the goals that majorly affect your life.

> Example of a general goal: "Study more each week"

> Example of a SMART goal: "Study for 3.5 hours per week"

Measurable: The second component of any SMART goal is its measurability. Making your goal measurable assures your progress. It assists you in making progress. When you measure your progress, you stay on track, reach your target dates, and experience achievement. By meeting you "little" goals, you become more excited at reaching your overall goal. Your goals should be motivational, methodical, and meaningful to assist you in achieving them.

> Example of a general goal: "Read more per week"

> Example of a SMART goal: "Read an additional 100 pages per week"

Attainable: The third component of any SMART goal is its attainability. Make your goals attainable in order to make them come true. By making them action oriented and achievable, you will actually attain your goal. When you set the goal, assess your group's attitudes, aptitudes, and financial capabilities to reach your goals. Set realistic time expectations for reaching your goals.

> Example of a general goal: "Go to the moon"

> Example of a SMART goal: "Build a 150 foot in diameter model of the moon"

Realistic: The fourth component of any SMART goal is its reality. To be realistic, a goal must represent an objective toward which you are both willing and able to work for. It is great to set a goal very high as long as you are able and willing to put the necessary time to reach the goal. Your goal should also be relevant so that you can continue to see the importance in reaching it.

> Example of a general goal: "Become the fastest runner"

> Example of a SMART goal: "Run a marathon in under 3 hours"

Timely: The final component of any SMART goal is its timeliness. Your goal should have some time parameters for its completion. You should make sure that your goal is trackable to make sure you are making progress towards your goal. You goal must be something that can be reached. Setting deadlines helps your brain to prioritize your goals.

> Example of a general goal: "Be able to curl 40 LBS"

> Example of a SMART goal: "Be able to curl 40 LBS by December 31st"

S.M.A.R.T. Goals. Adapted from "Constandse, Rodger. (2004). *SMART goals: how to set and achieve them*. Retrieved August 2008. http://www.timethoughts.com/goalsetting/smart-goals.htm.

Activities

Activity 3–1
Apply the learning styles discussed in this chapter and complete the following statements.

In the classroom, I learn best by

_____

In the classroom, I have difficulty learning when

_____

How will you use this information to perform better?

_____

Activity 3–2
Write down four words to describe your ideal self-concept.

1. _____

2. _____

3. _____

4. _____

What steps are necessary to make your ideal self-concept a reality?

_____

_____

Activity 3–3
What outside experiences and/or influences affect your educational behavior?

Outside Experiences and/or Influences.
1.
2.
3.
4.

Activity 3–4

Share the following information to introduce yourself to your classmates.

1. What is your name?

_____

2. Where were you born?

_____

3. What is your major (if you don't have one, what interests are you pursuing at school)?

_____

4. What is your favorite color?

_____

5. What is your favorite thing about attending school?

_____

6. If you could be any animal, what would it be and why?

_____

7. What else would you like us to know about you?

_____

Activity 3–5

Create three long-term goals in each section of your life plan. Make them realistic.

Personal	Career	Education
1.	1.	1.
2.	2.	2.
3.	3.	3.

Activity 3–6

Using the previous activities in this chapter, set long- and short-term goals. The star is your long-term goal. The steps are your short-term goals. Write positively and in detail. Set one personal goal and one career goal. Keep short-term goals specific, measurable, and realistic. Include what (the goal), when (specific time you plan to achieve it), and how to get there (be specific). Hint: Refer back to Cory's goal to obtain a car.

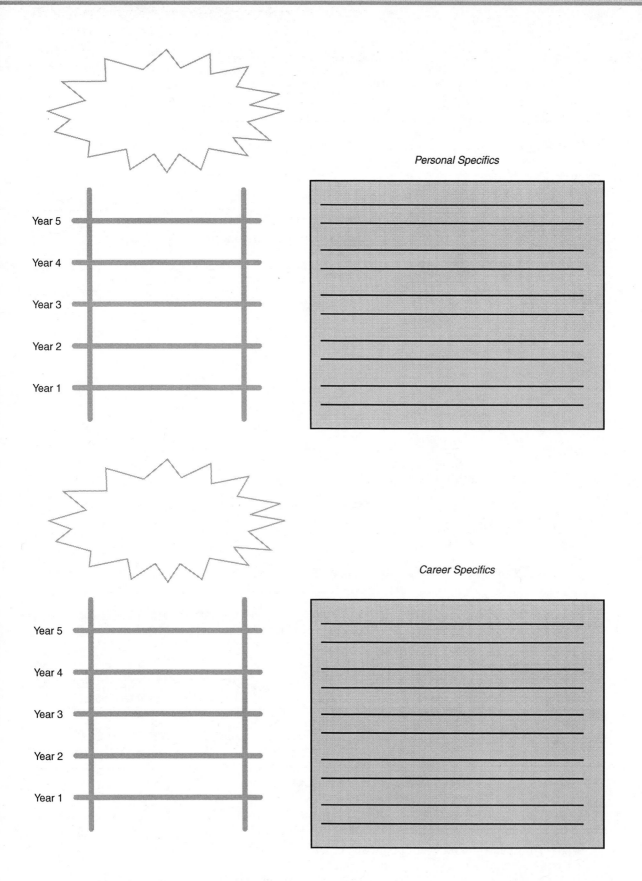

Personal Specifics

Year 5

Year 4

Year 3

Year 2

Year 1

Career Specifics

Year 5

Year 4

Year 3

Year 2

Year 1

1. The _____ identifies who you believe controls your future.

2. _____ is an individual's perception of how he or she views himself or herself, while _____ _____ is one's belief of how others view him or her.

3. When one understands one's own _____ and _____, it is much easier to understand reactions to others' actions.

4. A/An _____ affects group performance, which, in turn, impacts organizational performance.

5. Dealing with negative baggage involves _____ your past, _____, and moving _____ _____.

6. Past influences shape our _____

7. Goals need to be set so you can become _____.

8. Long-term goals are set to be reached after _____.

9. Short-term goals should usually be reached _____.

10. _____ help you reach long-term goals.

11. When setting a goal, there must be a time frame; it must be _____ _____ and _____.

12. _____ will help you decide what needs to be done and in what order.

13. To give up one thing for another is known as a/an _____.

14. Goals should be challenging but _____.

15. It is important to put goals into _____.

16. When creating a life plan, consider the following three areas:

_____

_____

_____

This writing assignment guides you through the process of creating goals. Remember that these goals must be realistic, attainable, important to you, and measurable. Be as specific as possible in every paragraph.

Identify and write your five-year and one-year career goals here. Identify what kind of job and what title you want, in what city you want to work, whom you want to work for, and why you chose this goal. Use the SMART method.

Five-Year Goal

Paragraph 1:	*In five years, I want to be . . .*

One-Year Goal(s)

Paragraph 2:	*In order to reach my five-year goal, I need to set the following short-term goals:*
	Identify necessary steps to reach your five-year goal. Be specific with activities, resources, and time frames.
Paragraph 3:	*I am currently...*
	What are you currently doing to reach these short-term goals? Be specific with activities, resources, and time frames.
Paragraph 4:	*I will know I have reached these goals when...*
	Goals must be measurable. How will you know when you have reached each short-term goal? Be specific with activities, resources, and time frames.
Paragraph 5:	*I need the following resources to reach my goal:*
	Identify physical, financial, emotional, and social resources and where they will come from.
Paragraph 6:	*My priorities for reaching my goals are:*
	Have priorities set for reaching your goals. Include your trade-offs and the areas where you may need to be flexible.

Time and Stress Management/ Organization Skills

by Lydia E. Anderson and
Sandra B. Bolt

We must use time as a tool, not as a crutch.

John F. Kennedy (1917–1963)

Objectives

- Describe how *stress* impacts workplace performance
- Identify the causes of stress and name methods of dealing with stress
- Deal with *procrastination* in a productive manner
- Apply *time management* techniques in the workplace
- Define the importance of organizing for optimal performance
- Apply organizational techniques in the workplace

How-Do-You-Rate

	Is your life in order?	Yes	No
1.	The inside of my car is clean.	☐	☐
2.	My personal workspace is free of clutter.	☐	☐
3.	My computer files are in order and it is easy to find documents.	☐	☐
4.	I maintain an address book (electronic or tradi-tional) to keep my professional network current.	☐	☐
5.	I make my bed every day.	☐	☐

If you answered "no" to two or more of these questions, it's time to get your life in order. Organization in all areas of your life decreases stress and improves time management—two factors that will contribute to workplace success.

The Impact of Stress on Performance

Walk into a workplace and you'll quickly form an impression of the work environment. Your first impression will most likely be based upon the demeanor of the employees and their interactions with each other. You will also notice if the work area is messy and unorganized or if it is clean and orderly. This chapter examines the influences that stress management, time management, and organization have on workplace productivity. We waste a lot of time looking for items that if arranged in an organized manner would make our jobs easier and save us time. When we fail to plan appropriately and do not have enough time to complete our work, we get stressed. Of course, there are other factors that contribute to a productive workplace, but time, stress, and organization are certainly major contributing forces. Stress management, time management, and organizational ability are personal skills that must be developed and consistently practiced. Positive personal habits spill into the workplace and become positive workplace behaviors.

Employers need employees who are healthy, relaxed, and well organized. Healthy employees are able to perform at their highest levels, have decreased absenteeism, and have fewer health claims than their unhealthy counterparts. Stress can impact workplace productivity, and stress is affected by factors including self-care matters such as diet and exercise and organizational issues like time management.

Stress is the body's reaction to tense situations. Stress can cause more than just a bad day. Constant stress can result in permanent mental and/or physical harm.

Although some forms of stress are beneficial and keep you mentally challenged, long-term (chronic) stress will eventually harm you in one way or another. It may start to affect your work performance and will most likely carry on to your personal life. While not all stress is within your control, try to maintain a low stress level. Stress-related losses are high and are costing organizations billions of dollars annually.

Types of Stress

You arrive in class and your teacher announces that today students are to give impromptu presentations on the lecture material. The students who are prepared and confident may be quite excited about the activity, while those who are not prepared or not confident may suddenly flush and feel their hearts racing. As a result they will be stressed. This illustration demonstrates that stressful situations vary from individual to individual. Stress is a normal part of life. What is important is that you recognize when you are stressed and deal with the stress appropriately. There is positive and negative stress. You will experience stress at school, at work, and at home. There is no avoiding it. However, how you react to and deal with stress determines how it will affect you. Some stress is minor and affects you at a specific time. This can be **positive stress.** Positive stress is a productive stress that provides the strength to accomplish a task. However, even positive stress can become negative if it continues and becomes problematic. For example, if you have a rushed deadline for a special project, your adrenaline will increase, giving you the mental and/or physical strength to finish the project on time. However, if you consistently have rushed deadlines, your stress level could increase and will eventually start working negatively on your mind and body.

Any stress can become **negative stress.** Becoming emotional or illogical or starting to lose control of your temper is a sign that you are experiencing unproductive or negative stress. This type of stress is continuous and may affect your mental and/or physical health. Negative stress commonly results in anger, depression, and/or distrust. Other signs of negative stress may include frequent headaches, fatigue, diminished or increased appetite, a poor immune system, or other physical weakness. Negative stress can ultimately result in ulcers, heart disease, or mental disturbances.

Cory has started experiencing headaches and fatigue lately. After thinking about recent activities, Cory realizes the headaches and fatigue may be a symptom of stress. With college and work, there seems to be no time for relaxation. Cory decides that this situation needs changing or the physical symptoms could get worse. Cory takes time to write out goals, make a plan, and practice stress management techniques. Soon after, Cory starts feeling better and has more control in balancing school and work, and has found free time to relax

Talk It Out

How can stress from school impact other areas of your life?

Talk It Out

What are common negative stressors students face, and what are positive responses?

Exercise 4-1   Recognize Your Stress

List at least three significant things that have happened to you in the last year that have caused you stress. Next to the stressor, include what happened to you mentally and/or physically.

Stressor	Symptoms of the Stressor (How You Respond Mentally and/or Physically)
1.	
2.	
3.	

Dealing with Stress

The first step in dealing with stress is to identify the key stressors in your life. Learning to both identify and deal with these stressors will reduce their negative effects. Be aware of them and how they affect your attitude and behavior. Life is not stress-free. The following steps will assist in not allowing stressful situations to get the best of you:

1. Identify the stressor. Find out what is causing you to be stressed.
2. Recognize why and how you are reacting to that stressor.
3. Take steps to better deal with the stress by visualizing and setting a goal for responding in a positive manner.
4. Practice positive stress relief.

The following are ways to relieve stress:

- Find an outlet to release tension. This can include daily exercise, a hobby, or some other healthy activity.
- Diminish (or ideally eliminate) the use of alcohol and/or drugs. These stimulants may cause mood swings that typically make matters worse.
- Do not become emotional. Becoming emotional means you are losing control and may become illogical in your response to the stress.
- Get organized. Take control of your workspace by eliminating unwanted clutter and prioritizing projects.
- Create and maintain a support network. Identify a few close friends and family members in whom you can confide and share concerns.
- Make time for yourself and learn to relax.
- Control your attitude and how you handle stressful situations.
- Eat a balanced diet and get plenty of sleep. Common results of sleep deprivation include anger, irritation, and exhaustion, all of which contribute to stress.
- Develop realistic goals.

Cory has been noticing that a coworker, Tammy, has been short-tempered and moody lately. Because Tammy is normally very pleasant to work with, Cory decides to ask her if something is wrong. Visiting with Tammy, Cory finds out that Tammy is being harassed by someone at work. She tells Cory how stressful this has been and that it is affecting her work and personal life. Cory encourages Tammy to take steps to stop this harassment. Cory also gives Tammy some tips to help deal with the stress. After a few weeks, Cory notices a positive change in Tammy. Dealing with the problem, along with using stress relievers, is helping Tammy get back to her pleasant self.

The key is to become aware of what is causing stress. Ignoring stress does not make it go away. Your body responds to stress. By being aware of what causes your stress, you can change how it will affect you.

Two final and important methods of managing stress include diet and exercise. A healthy physical body leads to a healthy mental mind. Consistently eat a balanced diet, including breakfast, lunch, and dinner. At these meals, balance protein, carbohydrates, vegetables, and fruit. Do not skip meals, especially breakfast.

Along with a balanced diet, exercise is a must. While you do not have to join a gym or lift weights, you do need to have a consistent exercise plan that gets your body moving. Exercise is a good way to clear your mind of troubles and

Talk It Out

What are ways you relieve stress?

increase creativity. There are simple ways to increase physical activity. Use the stairs instead of taking the elevator, or park your car a little farther away from a building to increase your walking distance. You don't have to spend an hour or more at a time; just exercising for ten minutes several times a day will increase energy and improve your health.

Exercise 4-2   What Have You Eaten in the Past Twenty-Four Hours?

A nutritious diet can make a difference in how you perform throughout the day and how you react to stressful situations. List what you have eaten in the past twenty-four hours. Decide whether or not it was nutritious.

What Have You Eaten?	Is It Nutritional?
1.	
2.	
3.	
4.	
5.	
6.	
7.	
8.	
9.	
10.	

The following is a list of simple physical activities that relieve stress. You probably do some of these things without realizing that they relieve stress.

- Enjoy leisure time
- Listen to music
- Relax
- Meditate and do deep breathing exercises
- Use positive visualization

Recognize what situations cause stress. If you recognize stressful situations, you can better control them. The more organized you are, the better prepared you will be, thus reducing stress.

When at work, if you cannot surround yourself with positive people, then create a positive personal space. Find a private place where you can take a few minutes each day for yourself to relax. Realize that people are not always going to agree with you at the workplace. There may be annoying people, and there may be people with whom you may not have a positive relationship. You may

Web Quiz

Take the online quiz to rate your current stress level or research ways to reduce stress levels.

http://www.arc.sbc.edu/stressquiz.html

find yourself in situations that become very stressful. Use the stress relief tools mentioned earlier in this chapter and make the best of the situation. Only you can control you attitude and your response to situations.

Take time outside of work to relax. Do not bring work troubles home with you, nor take home troubles to work. When you recognize your stressors and take care of yourself, you can reduce and/or eliminate the harm stress can do to you both at home and at work.

Check if your company has an Employee Assistance Program (EAP) and use it to get professional help. Typical employee assistance programs offer help with financial, legal, and psychological issues.

Job burnout is a form of extreme stress where you lack motivation and no longer have the desire to work. Signs of job burnout include:

- Being frequently tardy or absent
- Continually complaining
- Exhibiting poor physical and emotional health
- Lacking concern for quality
- Clock-watching and being easily distracted
- Gossiping
- Demonstrating a desire to cause harm to the company (theft of or damage to property)

If you have seriously tried to improve the current work situation and still find yourself at a dead end, you may need to consider a job change. Continuing in a job in which you have not been motivated in for a long period of time is destructive not only to you, but also to your company and coworkers.

Time Management

Recall the earlier scenario where the teacher assigned impromptu presentations on the lecture material and some students were stressed while others were not. Perhaps the stressed students were stressed because they did not study and therefore were not prepared. There is a clear link between stress and time management. There is also a link between time management and success. **Time management** is how you manage your time. Sometimes it seems there are never enough hours in the day. In business, time is money. The ability to use time wisely is a skill in itself. This skill is needed in the workplace. When you use your time efficiently, your tasks will be completed on time, and sometimes even early. Focus on tasks at hand and pay attention to details needed to do the job right the first time. If you are being more efficient and paying attention, your employer sees that you care about your job and are organized. In turn, this may lead to higher pay and/or a promotion.

Without proper time management skills, you may forget, lose, or spend more time than needed on an important project. Proper time management at work frees up more time for other activities both at work and at home. Make the effort to control your time.

You may get stressed at work because you do not have enough time to complete a project. However, many work projects are similar in nature and can therefore be managed easily. Prior to starting a project, make a plan. Set priorities and get organized. Do not wait until the last minute. If you have similar projects, create a template so you are not starting over with each project.

Rushing through a job typically results in errors that will only take more time to correct. Focus on completing a job right the first time.

A common workplace interruption is that of individuals who visit your work area and stay longer than necessary. When dealing with these individuals, always be professional and polite. Inform the individual that although you would like to visit, you have work that must be completed. If you are in an office environment, do not sit down nor invite your office visitor to take a seat. Standing by the door or entry to your workspace, politely tell your visitor that you are busy and unable to visit. Avoid having items such as a candy dish on your desk that attract unwanted guests. Further discussion of the use of body language and communication will be presented in later chapters.

Use activity 4-1 at the end of this chapter to identify how you spend your time. The following tips will help you organize and control your time:

1. Make a list of tasks for each day and prioritize that list; this is commonly referred to as a *to-do list*. Many PCs and smart phones offer task applications to make electronic lists. This is the electronic version of using a sticky note.
2. Keep a calendar accessible at all times. List all appointments, meetings, and tasks on your personal calendar. The calendar can be electronic or traditional.
3. Organize your work area. Use file folders and in-boxes to organize and prioritize projects.
4. Practice a one-touch policy. After you have looked at a project, letter, memo, or other item, file it, place it in a priority folder, forward it to the appropriate individual, or throw it away. Do not pile papers on your desk.
5. Avoid time wasters. Time wasters are small activities that take up only a small amount of time but are done more frequently than you may realize. These include unnecessary visiting or inappropriate activities such as personal texting or updating your social network site.
6. If possible, set aside time each day to address all communication at once, as opposed to handling messages as they arrive (e.g., e-mail and phone messages).
7. Do not be afraid to ask for help. Asking for help is not a sign of weakness or inefficiency if you are practicing sound time management techniques.

Exercise 4-3   Avoid Time Wasters

List time wasters you have experienced in the past few weeks. How did these time wasters affect your productivity? What change should be made?

Time Waster	How Did It Affect Productivity?	What Will You Improve?
1.		
2.		
3.		

Cory has learned to save time by answering some memos in a unique way. When Cory receives a memo that requires only a short response, instead of creating a new memo, Cory writes a response on the original memo. After writing the answer and making a copy for record, Cory sends the memo back. This procedure has saved Cory time.

Some individuals procrastinate and delay performing priority tasks. **Procrastination** is putting off tasks until a later time. This poor habit severely impedes time management and contributes to stress. People procrastinate for many reasons, including fear of failure, perfectionism, disorganization, or simply not wanting to perform the task because it is not pleasant. To overcome procrastination, first visualize the completed task. Knowing your end result and how you will feel when it is completed will motivate you to get started. The next step is to make a plan for completion by identifying what information and resources are required for the end result you envisioned. List every activity and piece of information you will need. After you have made your plan, get to work. If the task appears overwhelming, break it down into smaller tasks and complete each task in priority order. Breaks and celebrations are not only essential, but encouraged when you are working on a big project.

Cory was taking a chemistry class in which the instructor assigned a semester-long research project. When the project was assigned at the start of the semester, the instructor encouraged the students to make a plan and schedule dates to complete sections of the research throughout the semester so as to produce a quality project. Cory struggled with the class material and procrastinated working on the assignment. Unfortunately, as the semester wore on, Cory became immersed with other courses, a job, and personal issues and kept delaying the research project. The more Cory thought about the project, the more stressed Cory became. Finally, two weeks before the end of the semester, the instructor reminded the class that all research projects were due the day before the final. Cory realized there was no time to properly study for exams and also complete the research project. The procrastination resulted in Cory being stressed and receiving a failing grade in the chemistry course, because Cory gave up and did not even attempt to write the paper or take the final exam.

One final issue that contributes to both stress and poor time management is the inability for individuals to say "no" to co-workers, bosses, or others. At work, our goal is to be as productive as possible by prioritizing our current workload. Overcommitting ourselves risks compromising quality for quantity.

Exercise 4-4   What Went Wrong?

Based on what you have learned so far in our discussion of stress and time management, detail what Cory could have done to produce a better outcome in the chemistry class.

When you are pressed for time and someone asks you to assist with a project, first evaluate if the project is part of your primary work duties. If you have time and it does not conflict with your priority projects, agree to take on the new project. If you do not have time and you have greater priorities, decline the project. If it is your boss that is making the request, politely inform your boss that you want to help wherever and whenever possible, but you are currently working on another priority project and ask him or her which project should take precedent. Many bosses are unaware of an individual's workload at any given time, so your goal is to communicate your current priorities.

Talk It Out

How can you apply what you just learned regarding time management to your school performance?

Organizing and Performance

Individuals who are organized operate around goals and have learned that being surrounded by clutter deters focus. Organized individuals arrange their belongings in their home and work environments in a manner that reflects their goals. Establish a life plan and create goals to support this plan. Your life plan details what you want to accomplish and by when. Have your personal and work environment reflect your life plan, priorities, and values. Getting organized for optimal performance is not difficult. Being organized will not only optimize performance, but will also help you use your time more efficiently and reduce stress.

Follow these steps to get organized:

1. Take inventory. If you don't need it, donate it or throw it away. If an item is necessary but not used often, store it.
2. Place items where they are required. For example, keep printer paper by the printer, notepad and paper near the phone.
3. Avoid piles and miscellaneous folders. Although the intention is to get to a pile of information or a miscellaneous file sometime in the future, this rarely happens.
4. Return a used item to its appropriate area.
5. Routinely de-clutter. Organization skills are learned habits that must be reinforced. If you create a clean space and fail to keep it clean, you end up with a messy space.

While it may take time to organize, the time you invest in cleaning and organizing your space will release much more time for you to accomplish your goals. An organized and clutter-free area is calming and allows you to focus.

Tools for getting organized in the workplace can also be used at home. Technology has made it easier to get organized with electronic devices. However, there are other common organization tools to use, including shredders, filing, and the appropriate arrangement of desk space.

One of the easiest ways to get organized is to use a calendar. There are many calendaring options, including a computerized calendar, a mobile calendar, and a traditional paper calendar. For efficiency, businesses prefer an electronic calendar for computer networking purposes. It is common to have access to a computerized information manager on the web, a communications program on a computer, and/or a mobile device. Determine which type of calendar works best for your work situation; sometimes the solution is to use more than one that can be synced. Once you have determined which option is best for you, make a commitment to record all work-related and personal meetings and important deadlines. If your personal information manager and communications program is electronic, store telephone numbers, e-mail addresses, and other important messaging data in the program for easy access. Tasks, to-do lists, and notes can also be monitored and updated. Keep data current by immediately recording changes. If you use multiple organization tools, make a habit of transferring information on a daily basis. For maximum efficiency, customize applications to suit your needs.

Other ways to keep organized and improve performance is to check and answer your phone messages and e-mails at regular intervals. It is inefficient to return each phone message or e-mail as it comes in. The only exception to this is if there is an important message or e-mail that needs to be sent or answered immediately. Also break down larger tasks into simpler, smaller ones. When you break down tasks, you can space out projects. This enables you to organize the time needed to complete each task before starting the next. Again, the exception to this is if you have a priority task that needs to be completed immediately.

If you are assigned a personal workspace, keep your work environment and desk clean and clutter-free. Having no more than two personal items on a desk will maintain a professional look. Keep frequently used work tools easily accessible, including a stapler, tape, a notepad, pens, pencils, paperclips, scissors, a ruler, a calculator, highlighters, and a computer storage device. In addition, the use of a small bulletin/whiteboard for posting important reminders will help you keep track of important tasks and appointments. Have a trash can close to your desk, and throw away supplies that have been used or do not work anymore. Shred confidential materials at least once a day.

When managing paper files, maintain these files properly in a file cabinet and keep files neatly arranged in clearly labeled file folders. Keep dated documents in chronological order (most recent first). Other files can be arranged by subject or alphabetically. Be consistent in your filing method. Routinely used files should be easily accessible. Keep files updated, and be sure to dispose of old files properly. Any unnecessary files with personal information or identification numbers are considered confidential and should be shredded. If files are not important and do not have identification, they may be thrown in the trash.

For efficiency and security purposes, keep electronic files organized. Your computer desktop should contain only shortcuts to frequently used programs and files that you are currently working with. Routinely clean your computer desktop and keep it clutter-free. Just as with paper files, electronic files should be well organized and labeled. Establish folders for major projects, committees, and other items related to your job. Place appropriate documents inside each major project folder. Whenever possible, create subfolders for large projects so that you can properly file and quickly retrieve documents when necessary. Keep both folder and file names simple and easily identifiable. Also remember to routinely back up and/or secure your files to protect confidential information. Effective organization includes the proper handling of both electronic and paper mail. Your job may include sorting and/or opening mail. Use a letter opener to open all paper mail at one time. After opening the paper mail, sort it into piles. Throw away or shred junk mail immediately after opening. Respond to the sender of the mail if needed, file the document, or forward the mail to the appropriate party within the company. Do not open mail that is marked confidential unless instructed to do so. Mail should be kept private and not shared with co-workers. If you encounter a piece of mail that should be confidential, place it in a separate envelope and mark it confidential. Company letterhead or postage is not for personal mail.

Workplace Dos and Don'ts

Do recognize your stressors	*Don't* allow stress to make you mentally or physically sick
Do deal with stress appropriately	*Don't* think that stress will just go away
Do eat a balanced diet and have an exercise plan	*Don't* skip breakfast
Do manage your time by setting priorities and getting organized	*Don't* be afraid of asking for help when getting behind
Do take time to get organized	*Don't* give in to time wasters

Concept Review and Application

Summary of Key Concepts

- Stress is a physical, chemical, or emotional factor that causes bodily or mental tension
- Stress can be positive and/or negative
- Signs of stress include becoming emotional or illogical or losing control of your temper
- The first step in dealing with stress is to identify the stressor
- A balanced diet along with exercise will help you to better manage stress
- There are many ways to reduce stress, such as setting goals, relaxing, and getting enough sleep
- Good time management comes from being organized
- Avoid procrastination
- Being organized will optimize your performance and reduce stress

Key Terms

job burnout   negative stress   positive stress
procrastination   stress   time management

If You Were the Boss

1. You have noticed that an employee frequently is calling in sick and appears agitated when at work. What do you do?
2. You have just become the supervisor for a new department. What can you do to make the department and its employees more organized? Discuss appointment tools, necessary equipment, and software.

Video Case Study: Time Management and Organization Tips

This video presents expert advice on time management and workplace organization. To view these videos, visit the Student Resources: Professionalism section in www.mystudentsuccesslab.com. Then answer the following questions.

1. Name three reasons why time management and workplace organization is important.
2. Share three time management tools.
3. Share three organization tools you should practice in your personal work area.
4. Define *time wasters* and explain how to deal with them.

Web Links

http://www.mindtools.com/smpage.html
http://www.cdc.gov/niosh/topics/stress
http://www.effective-time-management-strategies.com
http://www.studygs.net/timman.htm

Activities

Activity 4–1

Your instructor will distribute a time log, use this log to keep track of how you spend your time for the next twenty-four hours. Track exactly how your time was spent. At the end of the time period, identify specific time wasters.

Identify three time wasters from your time log.
1.
2.
3.

Activity 4–2

In addition to what was mentioned in the chapter, research physical responses generated by prolonged stress. List your findings.

1.	4.
2.	5.
3.	6.

Activity 4–3

Conduct additional research and identify tips for relieving work stress. List them and explain how they help relieve stress.

Tip for Relieving Stress at Work	How Does It Help?
1.	1.
2.	2.
3.	3.
4.	4.

Activity 4–4

Identify the workplace effects of good and bad time management.

Effects of *Good* Time Management	Effects of *Bad* Time Management
1.	1.
2.	2.
3.	3.
4.	4.
5.	5.

1. Stress is a physical, chemical, or emotional factor that causes tension and may be a factor in

   _____.

2. Stress can be positive and/or _____.

3. The first step in dealing with stress is to _____.

4. Some ways to relieve stress include (choose four): _____,

   _____, _____, and

   _____.

5. Realizing your stressors and taking care of yourself will reduce or eliminate

   _____.

6. Managing time when you do not seem to have enough hours in the day is _____.

7. Being organized can _____ your performance.

Phase II: The Leader Who Understands Others

Motivation, Leadership, and Teams

by Lydia E. Anderson and Sandra B. Bolt

The price of greatness is responsibility.

Sir Winston Churchill (1874–1965)

81

Objectives

- Identify the characteristics of effective *leadership*
- Identify leadership styles
- Describe ways to develop leadership skills
- Define a *team* and its function
- Identify the characteristics of a team player
- Describe the elements of successful presentations and meetings

How-Do-You-Rate

	What kind of team member are you?	Yes	No
1.	Co-workers would say that I consistently behave in a professional manner at work.	☐	☐
2.	I normally arrive at least five minutes early to meetings.	☐	☐
3.	When participating in team projects, I always complete my portion of the project on time.	☐	☐
4.	If there is conflict within the team, I work to resolve the team conflict.	☐	☐
5.	I consistently behave as a leader in work-related situations, including knowing when to lead and knowing when to follow.	☐	☐

If you answered "yes" to two or more of these questions, congratulations. You display both leadership and positive team member behaviors.

A Foundation for Performance

The three elements of motivation, leadership, and teamwork create the foundation for productivity and organizational success. You do not have to have a leadership title to exhibit leadership behaviors. Employees should display the characteristics of a leader because they have the opportunity to lead. In addition to motivation and leadership, teamwork will be discussed. These three elements are intertwined, and they also require skill in understanding how to work with others who may or may not be motivated, be a part of your team, or want to lead.

Teams and Performance

Most individuals have experienced being part of a successful team. Perhaps it was a sports team, or maybe it was in school when a group of students successfully completed a big project. Whatever the task, individuals were part of a unit whose members shared a goal and respected one another. These important factors resulted in success. Learning to get along with others is a skill that is necessary in the workplace. You will most likely be working with others in a group or as part of a team. Each team should strive toward creating synergy. **Synergy** is defined as two or more individuals working together and producing more than the sum of their individual efforts. When people are truly working together as a team, performance is at a premium and the result exceeds what each individual could do alone. This section discusses teamwork, factors vital for team success, and the impact teams have on an organization's overall performance.

It is becoming increasingly common for companies to rely on teams to accomplish goals. A **team** is a group of people linked to a common purpose. In today's workplace, you will most likely work in a team. The team will be assigned the task of reaching a goal. In a team setting, each member shares a common goal, and members are accountable to one another and to the organization as a whole. Because members share accountability, teams provide opportunities for members to take a leadership role in helping the team successfully reach its goal. In a team setting, each team member has a sense of ownership for the team's performance. This can occur only when team members are active participants and are accountable to fellow team members.

Several types of teams exist at work. Teams that occur within the organizational structure are formal teams. **Formal teams** are developed within the formal organizational structure and include functional teams (e.g., individuals from the same department) or cross-functional teams (individuals from different departments). **Informal teams** are composed of individuals who get together outside of the formal organizational structure to accomplish a goal. Examples of informal teams include a company softball team and a group of coworkers collecting food for a local charity. Another type of team that is common in today's workplace is the virtual team. **Virtual teams** are teams that function through electronic communications because they are geographically dispersed. It is quite common for virtual teams to operate in various time zones and across national borders. Effective communication and pre-meeting planning is essential when working in a virtual team. Refer to Chapter 9 for additional information on effective communication and appropriate use of communication technologies.

No matter what type of team situation you are involved with, you need to get along with your team members and behave professionally. Your performance for getting the job done depends on this team effort. A team composed of individuals who behave professionally performs better.

Teams go through five stages of team development: forming, storming, norming, performing, and adjournment. In the **forming stage,** you are getting to know and form initial opinions about team members. Assumptions are based on first impressions. Sometimes these impressions are right; other times, they are wrong. In stage two, the **storming stage,** some team members begin to have conflict with each other. When team members accept other members for who they are (i.e., overcome the conflict), the team has moved into the **norming stage.** It is only then that the team is able to enter the **performing stage,** where they begin working on the task. Once the team has completed its task, it is in the **adjourning stage,** which brings closure to the project. Note that it is normal for a team to go through these phases. As a team member, expect and accept when your team is moving through each phase. Some teams successfully and rapidly move through the forming, storming, and norming phases and get right to work (performing), while other teams cannot get beyond the initial phases of forming or storming. Make every effort to move your team along to the performing stage, and recognize that minor conflicts are a part of team development. Successful teams move beyond the conflict and accept each member for his or her unique talents and skills.

You may work with team members you know and see every day in the work-place. However, you may have to work with a team of people you have never met before. Some team members may be from your immediate department (functional teams), some may be from outside of your department (cross-functional teams), and some may be from outside of the company. Good people skills and a willingness to lead are what make individuals valuable team members.

In a team situation, you will usually have your own job to perform, but you are also accountable to your fellow team members. The success of others within the company depends on how you do your job. Although you may be working independently from your team members, it is still important that you complete your job done on time and correctly. An effective team member is able to work with everyone on the team. You may have to work with a person with whom you do not care to work. No matter what disagreements you may have, get along with this person and be professional at all times. This is a skill needed for any job.

Characteristics of a Team Member

Common team projects include improving product quality, providing excellent customer service, and creating and/or maintaining company records. A good team member is one who does his or her job in a manner that is contributing to the project's goal. This means good team members are trustworthy, are efficient, and communicate at all times.

As a team member, know the objectives and goal of the team. The activity performed for your team should support the team's objectives and goal. When there is a team working on a specific project, there is a goal, so the first step for effective teams is to set objectives to reach that goal. Do not just jump into a project without a clear understanding of the expected outcome. It is also important to not reinvent the wheel or waste time and money. The best way to avoid these common mistakes is to solicit ideas and input from all team members.

Once the team has identified its goal and objectives, the team can identify various alternatives for how best to successfully achieve the goal. One popular way of doing this is through brainstorming. **Brainstorming** is a problem-solving method that involves identifying alternatives that allow members to freely add ideas while other members withhold comments on the alternatives. Brainstorming is successful because it is fast and provides members the opportunity to contribute different and creative ideas. Brainstorming starts with the presentation of a problem, such as how to improve office communication. Members then have a set time to make any suggestion for improving office communication. The suggestions can be obvious (e.g., a newsletter) or fun and creative (have a daily off-site office party). No matter the suggestion, members are to withhold comment and judgment on the idea until the brainstorming session is over. In effective brainstorming sessions, even an off-the-wall comment such as the suggestion to have a daily off-site office party may spark a more practical idea that contributes to solving the problem (e.g., have a company-wide gathering).

Although conflict is a natural part of team development, occasionally there are teams that are filled with hard-to-resolve conflict. Do not let one member ruin the synergy of a team. If possible, confidentially pull the member aside and ask that person what it is about the team or project that he or she finds objectionable. Also ask the team member how he or she feels the issue can best be resolved. Calmly and logically help the individual work through the issues. Accept the fact that he or she may not (1) recognize there is a problem, (2) openly share the reason for the conflict, or (3) want to come to a solution. If you or others on the team attempt to solve the problem with the difficult team member and he or she rejects the effort, your team needs to move forward without that person. One team member should not have so much power that he or she negatively affects the efforts of the entire team. Although team conflict is a natural stage of team development, it should not cripple a team. When the problem team member is not around, do not allow other team members to talk negatively about the individual. Your job is to be a productive, positive team member who assists in successfully accomplishing the team's goal.

In addition to knowing the goals of the project and what your specific roles and responsibilities are in the team effort, know the responsibilities of all the other team members. Whenever possible, identify ways to support other team members and assist them in accomplishing the team's objectives. Take responsibility to attend all team meetings and be on time. Participation, sharing, support, understanding, and concern are all part of serving on a team. During team meetings, be involved in discussions and determine what work is needed for accomplishing the goal. Do not be afraid to speak up during team meetings. Some of your ideas may not be considered, but that does not mean they are not important. Be responsible, and finish assignments in a timely manner. As a team, review all aspects of the project together before completing the project. Remember, team members are accountable to one another.

Cory's department was having problems meeting its production goal. The manager asked selected members of the department to form a team and create a plan for increasing production. Cory volunteered to serve on this team. It was the first team project Cory had been involved in, and did not know what to expect. Fortunately, Cory had a good team leader. The team leader sat down with the team and helped identify a team goal and objectives so that members knew exactly what needed to be done and who would be responsible for each activity. At the next meeting, the team leader led a brainstorming session. Some good ideas were shared. Cory had an idea but was afraid to speak up, thinking the idea might not be as good as the others. Remembering that members need to freely add ideas during brainstorming, Cory decided to share an idea. It turned out the team liked the idea, and it became an important part of the project plan.

Communication is a key element of effective teamwork. Do not make assumptions about others or a team project. If you have questions regarding any aspect of a project, respectfully speak up. Earlier in this chapter, you learned that it is normal for teams to experience conflict. If others do not agree

Exercise 5-1   Brainstorm for Saving

Brainstorm as many ideas as possible to help you and/or your classmates save money while going to college.

Exercise 5-2 Good Team Member Characteristics

Name the two most important characteristics you would want to see in your team members and explain why.

Characteristics	How Does this Help the Team Achieve Success?
1.	
2.	
3.	

with your ideas, keep a positive attitude. If your team takes a wrong turn, do not waste time on blame; take corrective action and learn from any mistakes that are made. Each team member should be able to state his or her position and ideas, and it should then be a team effort to decide which ideas to use. Do not assume that any team member's idea will not be worth hearing. The whole point of a team project is to get as many ideas as possible in order to come up with the best solution for reaching the goal. If the team makes a decision with which you did not agree, you have expressed and explained your objection, and the team still decides to continue, support the team's decision and keep assisting the team in achieving its goal. Conflict is a normal part of teamwork. Learn to work through conflict. This is where open, honest, and timely communication with all team members is important.

Be an active participant on your team. Do not allow team members to do your work because you know they will do it for you. Sometimes in a team situation, one member contributes nothing because that member knows others will do the work. If you have a lazy team member, continue to do your best and try to work around that person. Try talking to the poorly performing team member and identify why he or she is not doing his or her share. If the team member provides a good reason, suggest that he or she excuse himself or herself from the team. If the team member simply refuses to perform, you may need to decide as a team to have the unproductive team member dismissed or replaced.

Meetings

A common form of team interaction and workplace communication is a meeting. Meetings are either informational, discussion driven, decisional, or some combination of the three. Meetings can be formal or informal. The most common form of meetings in the workplace is a department meeting, which is when a boss formally meets with his or her employees.

Prior to meetings, a **meeting agenda** is normally distributed to all attendees. A meeting agenda is an outline of major topics and activities that are scheduled to be addressed during the meeting. Some agendas have time limits attached to each item. If you receive an agenda prior to a meeting, take time to read the agenda and become familiar with the topics of discussion. If there is an item you would like placed on the agenda, notify the person in charge of the meeting. If you are responsible for an agenda item, plan what you are going to share and/or request prior to the meeting. Prepare handouts for each attendee if necessary.

The most common type of meeting is a face-to-face meeting where all parties are physically present in one location. When you arrive at a face-to-face meeting, arrive early. Depending on the size of the meeting, there can be one table, or many tables filled with meeting attendees. If there is a head table, do not sit at the head table unless you are invited to do so. If there are no assigned seats and you are speaking, sit toward the front of the room. The **meeting chair** is the individual who is in charge of the meeting and has prepared the agenda. This person normally sits at the head of the table. If the chair has an assistant, the assistant will usually sit at the right side of the meeting chair. Other individuals in authority may sit toward the front of the table, or they will sit at the opposite end of the table. If you are unsure of where to sit at a conference table, wait to see where others sit, and then fill in an empty seat.

It is not only important, but respectful for employees to show up on time and be prepared for meetings. Most formal business meetings will follow some form of **Robert's Rules of Order,** a guide to running meetings. Robert's Rules of Order is oftentimes referred to as parliamentary procedure. At the start of a meeting, the meeting chair will call the meeting to order and, if appropriate, review the minutes from the last meeting. After the review of minutes, the meeting chair will ask that the minutes be approved. Once the minutes are approved, the agenda issues will be addressed in the agenda order. At the close of the meeting, the meeting chair will adjourn the meeting.

As a meeting participant, take your turn speaking by contributing thoughtful and relevant information when appropriate. Keep your discussion to the topic at hand and assist the meeting chair by keeping the discussion moving, with all contributions being professional, respectful, and focused on the goals of the company.

When distance separates meeting participants, virtual meetings take place. These meetings occur through the use of technology such as videoconferencing, telephone, or the Internet. A discussion on professional behavior related to these electronic communication venues is presented in Chapter 9.

Team Presentations

Some work situations require employees to create and provide a presentation as a team. The presentation material provided in Chapter 7 also applies to team presentations. When working with others, the first step is for all team members to agree upon the presentation goal. The team should then create the presentation outline. Using the outline as a foundation, discuss and agree upon the verbal, visual, and support content. Just as with other team situations, each member needs to take responsibility and be accountable to one another. Do not just split up sections and piece a presentation together at the last minute. Team presentations must be completed and reviewed by the entire team before presenting. Demonstrating positive human relation skills is a key to the success of a team. Each member must communicate, share duties, and behave in a respectful and professional manner.

Workplace Dos and Don'ts

Do be an active participant by being accountable to fellow team members	*Don't* ignore the needs of others in the workplace
Do be a good team member by being trustworthy and efficient and by communicating at all times	*Don't* leave the leadership process up to others
Do express yourself during team meetings	*Don't* think your ideas are not of value
Do recognize that people are motivated by different factors	*Don't* ignore team meetings and deadlines
Do make every effort to increase your leadership skills	*Don't* allow negative team members to disrupt the team's performance

Concept Review and Application

Summary of Key Concepts

- Everyone has the ability to become a successful leader
- Most companies use teams to accomplish goals
- An effective team comprises individuals who share a goal and respect for one another
- A good team member is one who does his or her job in a manner that is productive toward the end project
- Although team conflict is a natural stage of team development, do not allow conflict to cripple a team
- Communication is a key element of effective teamwork

Key Terms

adjourning stage

forming stage

leadership

meeting chair

norming stage

Robert's Rules of Order

synergy

teams

informal teams

performing stage

brainstorming

formal teams

meeting agenda

motivation

storming stage

virtual teams

If You Were the Boss

1. You have assembled a group of employees into a team to reach the goal of improving customer service in your department, but all they do is argue when they meet. What should you do?

2. Your employees have successfully met their production goals this week. Based on Maslow's hierarchy of needs, how can you motivate them to meet next week's goals?

Web Links

http://www.nwlink.com/~donclark/leader/leadhb.html

http://www.associatedcontent.com/article/317564/theimportance_of_teamwork_in_the_workplace.html

http://www.accel-team.com/human_relations/hrels_02_maslow.html

http://www.deepermind.com/20maslow.htm

Activity 5–1

If you were teaching this class, what specific topics or activities could you include in the course to help students better meet each level of Maslow's hierarchy?

Level	Motivation Factor
Self-Actualization	
Esteem	
Social	
Safety	
Physiological	

Activity 5–2

Research President Abraham Lincoln and answer the following questions.

What key leadership qualities made him unique?

_____

_____

What challenges did he face?

_____

_____

How can you apply lessons learned from your President Lincoln research to your leadership development?

_____

_____

Activity 5–3

Write about a time when you belonged to a successful team. Identify at least three specific factors that made the team successful.

Team Success Factors
1.
2.
3.

Activity 5–4

Look up any two rules of Robert's Rules of Order online. Explain what you learned.

Rule	What you learned
1.	
2.	

Sample Exam Questions

1. _____ hierarchy of needs is used to explain _____.

2. Every team goes through _____: forming, _____, norming, _____, and _____.

3. _____ is a way for teams to identify various alternatives or solutions for how best to successfully achieve the goal.

4. A/An _____ is one who will work with others to help guide and motivate.

5. Communication with all team members must be _____, _____, and _____.

6. _____ is an internal drive; therefore, no one can motivate you. Others can provide only a _____ environment.

7. At work, _____ are based on trust, professionalism, and mutual respect.

Examples of Common Roles in Groups

Task Roles	Role Description	Example of Role in Use	Group-Building Roles	Role Description	Example of Role in Use
Information seeker	Aware that the group needs more facts or data before proceeding.	"We cannot vote on this yet; we need more information first, so let's ask Sharon to brief us at the next meeting."	Gatekeeper	Inviting those who have not yet spoken or who have been trying to say something into the conversation.	"Tanya has been trying to say something on this for a while—I'd like to hear what that is."
Opinion seeker	Aware that the group needs more insight, ideas, or opinions before proceeding.	"What do you think, Roger? You have had a lot of experience with this topic."	Encourager	Welcoming all individuals and diverse ideas. Responding warmly to promote the inclusion and empowerment of others.	"What the sophomores just said about this issue was really enlightening. I am really glad you took some risks to tell us that. Thanks."
Opinion giver	Sharing one's views, feelings, or ideas so the group has the benefit of one's thinking.	"I strongly think we must increase the budget for this project if we intend to serve more students.	Mediator	Harmonizing conflict and seeking to straighten out opposing points of view in a clear way.	"You two don't seem as far apart on this issue as it might seem. You both value the same thing and have many points of agreement."
Summarizer	Condensing the nature of the opinions or discussion in a capsule format for clarity.	"I strongly think we must increase the budget for this project if we intend to serve more students."	Follower	An active listener who willingly supports the group's actions and decisions.	"I haven't said much, but this has been a great discussion and I feel really informed. I am comfortable with the decision."
Clarifier	Elaborating or explaining ideas in new words to add meaning. Showing how something might work if adopted.	"Jim, did you mean we need more involve-ment, meaning quantity, or better involvement, like quality?"			

"Common Roles in Groups." Adapted from Komives, S.R., Lucas, N., and McMahon, T.R. (2007) *Exploring Leadership: For college students who want to make a difference* (2nd ed.). San Francisco: Jossey-Bass.

Relational Leadership and Stages of Group Development

When the group is . . .	Relational leadership philosophy would encourage participants to . . .
1. **Forming**—initial coming together of groups / teams	Be inclusive and empowering. Make sure all the shareholders and stakeholders are involved. Seek diverse members to bring talent to the group. Model the processes of inclusion and shared leadership. Identify common purposes and targets of change.
2. **Storming**—group work presents differences of opinion and no clear goals and purposes have been set; individuals assert themselves	Create a climate in which each person matters and build commitment to the group as a community of practice. Be ethical and open. Be patient, to give divergent views a full hearing. Be aware when you may be biased or blocking the full participation of another. Handle conflict directly and openly, encouraging participants to identify their biases. Revisit the purposes of the group and targets of change.
3. **Norming**—patterns of 'how work is done' emerge; procedures are established	Be fair with processes. Practice collaboration. Keep new members welcomed, informed, and involved. Clarify the individual's responsibility to and expectations of the group and the group's responsibilities to and expectations of individuals.
4. **Performing**—work gets done	Celebrate accomplishments and find renewal in relationships. Empower members to learn new skills and share roles in new ways to stay fresh. Revisit purposes and rebuild commitment.
5. **Adjourning**—closure of group work	Evaluate formatively and summatively; assess work. Recognize accomplishments.

Adapted from Komives, S.R., Lucas, N., and McMahon, T.R. (2007) *Exploring Leadership: For college students who want to make a difference* (2nd ed.). San Francisco: Jossey-Bass.

Understanding Others

by Susan R. Komives, Nance Lucas,
and Timothy R. McMahon

chapter **6**

Courtesy of Shutterstock.

Consider this situation:

Place yourself in a typical meeting of an organization in which you are a member. Have you ever found yourself wondering . . .

> Laurie wonders why the men in the organization seem to dominate the discussions.
>
> Martina wonders why some of the group's members never say anything.
>
> James wonders why some of his peers enjoy controversy so much. They seem to enjoy the disagreement and heated debate.
>
> Patrick wonders what it's like to be one of the few students of color in the room.
>
> Julianna wonders if the students in the organization who are gay feel safe.
>
> Angela wonders if those students who are very religious are offended by any of the conversations going on during the meeting.
>
> Martin wonders how they could get some international students interested in joining the organization.

What do you wonder about the motives and behavior of others when you're sitting in a typical organization meeting?

A central goal of understanding yourself is to develop a sense of awareness that can result in true community and common purpose with others. There are three central questions (Komives, 1994, p. 219) to ask yourself in any setting:

- How am I like no one else here?
- How am I like some others here?
- How am I like everyone here?

Each of us brings uniqueness and individuality to any situation. Your skills, background, and preferences create a unique person—you. But you are not alone. To be truly inclusive and empowering, you must also understand others. The importance of this cannot be overstated. As the nation becomes more diverse and the world becomes smaller and more connected through technology, it becomes "flatter" (Friedman, 2005). Understanding others is a necessity for all leaders.

Chapter Overview

This chapter briefly explores some characteristics of gender, ethnicity, and culture that illustrate how differences need to be understood as you work toward leadership that is inclusive and empowering. The chapter also explores various leadership processes—including communication, conflict resolution, and decision making—that are influenced by diverse approaches. The chapter concludes with a discussion of communication skills, such as empathy and assertiveness, that are useful in working effectively with others in leadership.

Individuality and Commonality

Other people might be similar to you or very different from you. Even if others look the same, they may have different values, preferences, or approaches to learning. Some of these differences in ourselves and others come from our gender, ethnicity, or culture; some come from our environments.

In the grand scheme of living human species, we are more alike than we are different. Research into the human genome has certainly confirmed this. Finding common human purpose is the focus on which to center our perceptions of difference. The poet Maya Angelou (1994) has remarkable insight into the commonalties of being human. In her poem "Human Family," she describes all of our uniqueness as people that set us apart, but concludes, "We are more alike, my friends, than we are unalike" (pp. 224–225).

In any group setting, you can look around and see others who look like you. You will see men or women, people with visible racial or ethnic characteristics, or people of different ages. Also, you might see people wearing symbolic attire like your own: a wedding ring, a sorority pin, a pink triangle, a Star of David, or tennis whites. You might also identify with others when they express ideas you agree with, share experiences you have had, or have goals you also hold, regardless of visible characteristics that might have initially made them seem unlike you. You may begin to find similarities of interests: being in the same major, living close together, thinking alike about current politics, working out daily, being parents, or being affiliated with the same religion. Finding some people like you creates a feeling of association called social identity and leads to the identification of subcommunities.

On a transcendent level, something binds you to everyone around you, no matter how different they may seem: you all want to learn the subject in a particular course; you all value the goals of the organization meeting you have attended, be it the residence hall association, the aikido club, or a Bible study class; or you all want to work toward a common purpose like changing the university's policy on weekend library hours. The challenge of leadership is coming to common purpose from the vast differences that individuals bring to a situation. Finding the purpose, vision, and common commitments that create a "we" from a group of individuals is the challenge of community.

"I believe that every individual can provide a new perspective on a situation. No matter what your experiences are, they are different from mine and therefore we see things differently. Using this perspective in addition to one's ideas allows for better communication, better solutions, and better leadership."—Cathy Ragan was formerly the student government president at Rowan University.

The English language may well be the only one that values the individual to such a degree that the word for the first person singular—*I*—is capitalized. This emphasis on the individual is grounded in a predominantly Western tradition. Those with non-Western roots may find it easier to envision *we* because those cultural traditions emphasize the collective, the family, or group. To truly establish a sense of *we*, the individual needs to let go of self enough to see the connections to others.

Buber (1958) encouraged an exploration of "I-Thou"; leadership educators have encouraged "I→you→we" (National Invitational Leadership Symposium, 1990). This might best be expressed symbolically by showing that the focus on the individual (I) needs to be de-emphasized (i) to truly listen and engage with another (you) as equals, so that all can move forward to become a community (we) (see Figure 6-1).

```
"I"  ⇒  "i"
          ⇑      ⇒   "we"
       "you"
```

Figure 6-1

I, You, and We

One challenge, then, is to understand yourself well enough to know how you are seen by others and to modify your own behaviors and attitudes to encourage a spirit of openness and connection with others. The second challenge is to engage in the hard work of understanding others so that together you can form meaningful community and engage in coalitions for group change.

Groups are made up of great diversity. Even if members are all of one sex or one race or one major, there are great differences in personality, learning preferences, and experiences. The pluralism of a group refers to the plethora of differences that need to be understood in order to accomplish shared purposes. Pluralistic leadership results when heterogeneous groups of people work together to accomplish change. Pluralistic leadership is enhanced when a person understands, develops an appreciation for, and possesses the skills needed to communicate across these borders and come to common understandings.

Understanding Gender Diversity

It is salient to ask yourself, How does my gender influence my attitudes and behaviors? How does my experience as a man or woman shape my worldview and how might it shape the worldview of others? Characteristics of gender differences are too numerous to develop fully, but it is important to realize that we all deal with both sex roles and gender roles. The two terms are often used interchangeably, but sex roles are those expectations resulting from biology, like pregnancy or muscle mass, whereas gender roles are socially constructed expectations that get labeled masculine or feminine.

Gender roles are often limiting and inaccurate when assigned to individual men and women. For example, although only women can bear children, women are not the only sex to be nurturing of children. Historically, men's involvement in the development of children has been limited because that role has been considered feminine and nurturing. Likewise, women may be athletic, but it has been hard for women to engage in sports that require high physical contact, like football and rugby, because those sports are considered masculine. Women who are not nurturing or men who are not athletic may suffer from gender role discrimination by acting or being different from conventional paradigms. Likewise, those who hold a conventional leadership expectation that leaders should be decisive, in charge, competitive, and self-reliant may be holding a traditional masculine paradigm that excludes many women, as well as many men who are very capable but who do not lead from that perspective.

From the beginnings of our lives, our gender role perceptions are shaped by the many messages we receive from the environment. Even those parents who make sure the storybooks their children read do not promote gender role or sex role stereotypes and who give dolls to their sons and trucks to their daughters soon realize that other socialization agents (like peers, toys, television, and conversations on the bus going to school every morning) reinforce traditional gender messages. Many boys learn to be tough, objective, unemotional, and competitive, and many girls learn to be polite, caring, emotional, and supportive.

To understand how men and women have come to be as they are, we can learn from children's development. The way we play in childhood establishes patterns of how we work and communicate as adults. Boys often play outside in rough-and-tumble games, and extraverted leaders shout commands in competitive settings. Winning or losing becomes very important. Most games are played using teams. Even inside games like video or computer games often have elaborate hierarchical systems with complex rules and procedures that involve dominating or annihilating enemies and are frequently preferred by boys. Girls, however, often play inside in calm settings with one another or with a small group of friends. Their play stresses intimacy and values social relationships. Many of their preferred games have no winners or losers but every person gets a turn. Such games are jumping rope, hopscotch, or playing house (Tannen, 1990).

The social learning that happens with play and many other experiences often leads females to seek and value intimacy and relationships, whereas males often seek and value independence.

Intimacy is key in a world of connection in which individuals negotiate complex networks of friendship, minimize differences, try to reach consensus, and value the appearance of superiority which would highlight differences. In a world of status, *independence* is key, because a primary means of establishing status is to tell others what to do, and taking orders is a marker of low status (Tannen, 1990, p. 26).

Think of how rare it is in entertainment to find people who play roles that are different from conventional gender roles. Can you think of a television show or movie in which a woman played a role traditionally viewed as being for a man? Or in which a man played a role traditionally reserved for a woman?

Childhood play experiences also contribute to the development of the thinking or feeling orientation described in Jungian preference types. Remember that there is great variation among men and among women, but these patterns do raise our awareness and understanding of differences.

Men and women tend to hold different attributions for their successes and failures. Many women tend to credit their successes to external factors like luck and being in the right place at the right time. They might say, "Oh, I don't deserve the credit. So many people helped." They credit their failures to internal factors like not being prepared or not having the right skills or not having enough time. Many men, in contrast, tend to credit successes to internal factors like being prepared and capable and attribute their failures to external factors like fate, others not doing their part, or bad luck.

However, "psychological and physiological data on sex-linked traits suggest that the degree of overlap between the sexes is as important, or more important, than the average differences between them" (Lipman-Blumen, 1984, p. 4). Both men and women are capable of making good decisions, leading effectively, being responsible group members, and communicating with clarity, but they may go about doing those things differently than the other sex would (Eagley, Karau, & Makhijani, 1995). The fact that we persist in observing differences speaks to the power relationships that continue to exist in which men's ways, views, and artifacts have had higher status. Because men have traditionally held many visible leadership positions, the conventional paradigm of leadership was often socially constructed as having these same male characteristics.

Expectations that limit people's range of roles and suppress their individuality will likely inhibit their effectiveness in their communities. Sex or gender, however, is only one identity perspective we bring to a situation. We all have other salient social identities that are based on attributes such as our culture, ethnicity, age, or sexual orientation.

Understanding Cultural Diversity

Culture encompasses everything about how a group of people thinks, feels, and behaves. It is their pattern of knowledge. It is a "body of common understandings" (Brown, 1963, p. 3). Culture is "the sum total of ways of living; including values, beliefs, esthetic standards, linguistic expression, patterns of thinking, behavioral norms, and styles of communication which a group of people has developed to assure its survival in a particular physical and human environment. Culture, and the people who are part of it, interact, so that culture is not static" (Hoopes & Pusch, 1979, p. 3). We may be so embedded in our culture that it is hard to see it clearly.

Culture is, therefore, a broad term that could be applied to an office or a campus, to aging, or to a group of people who share a common race or ethnicity. Many cultures coexist simultaneously in any group. Effective leaders need to develop an appreciation for multiculturalism to build inclusiveness, collaboration, and common purposes. A prerequisite to developing a greater sense of multiculturalism is the conscious awareness of culturally informed assumptions (Helms, 1992; Pedersen, 1988).

Culture has often been described in terms of race and ethnicity. We encourage you to be cautious about the construct of race. Race is a "somewhat suspect concept used to identify large groups of the human species who share a more or less distinctive combination of hereditary physical characteristics" (Hoopes & Pusch, 1979, p. 3). The California Newsreel entitled *Race—The Power of an Illusion* explores this concept in detail in this three-hour video series and presents evidence that the very concept of race has no biological foundation. According to their web site,

> The division of the world's peoples into distinct groups—"red," "black," "white," or "yellow" peoples—has became so deeply imbedded in our psyches, so widely accepted, many would promptly dismiss as crazy any suggestion of its falsity. Yet, that's exactly what this provocative three-hour series by California Newsreel claims. *Race—The Power of an Illusion* questions the very idea of race as biology, suggesting that a belief in race is no more sound than believing that the sun revolves around the earth. Yet race still matters. Just because race doesn't exist in biology doesn't mean it isn't very real, helping shape life chances and opportunities. (http://www.newsreel.org/nav/title.asp?tc=CN0149)

As noted educator Derald Wing Sue (2003) states, "Many difficulties exist, however, in using race as a descriptor" (p. 34).

Yet, historically, race has been a very powerful aspect of life in the United States and continues to impact every campus today. It has been used to marginalize whole groups of people, and students on campuses experience racism every day. The Relational Leadership Model, with its emphasis on inclusion and empowerment, embraces the belief that the group, team, organization, community, nation, and world will be made better when all participants are heard, made visible, and valued for their contributions.

Historically, the dominant culture—the culture in the powerful majority—has not had to examine its beliefs and practices because it is not disadvantaged by them. The majority norms often became the standards used to judge others who are not in the majority. America's attention to racial and ethnic diversity has led to new awareness of what it means to be White and of European origin in the American culture. Peggy McIntosh (1989) coined the phrase the "invisible knapsack" to describe the concept of "White privilege." This weightless knapsack is filled with provisions that help you travel through life more easily. Even well-meaning people in the majority culture often take for granted the benefits of White privilege, which include shopping without being followed, being able to buy or rent housing of their choice, and easily finding toys and pictures that look like themselves (Talbot, 1996). In a general sense, it is useful to think of the privileges afforded any of us by virtue of personal characteristics that place us in a powerful "majority" (for example, being male, heterosexual, able-bodied, educated, financially comfortable) and examine closely how unconsciously affirming the privileges associated with those characteristics may actually cause or influence the oppression of others, even though oppression is unintended. Cris Cullinan (1999) describes privilege in a slightly different way. She notes that people with privilege are presumed to be innocent, worthy, and competent. We must examine how the characteristics of these forms of privilege may be attached to our expectations of what it means to be a leader or to not be a leader, and we must learn to value, or at least recognize, that leadership may take on different characteristics.

Understanding International Diversity

Understanding how to work with persons from other countries is even more complex but can be an exciting and rewarding experience. At times, it can also be very challenging. One of the great opportunities afforded to college students is the chance to get to know and work with students from other nations and, if you have the opportunity, to study abroad. As Javidan and House (2001) noted in describing global leaders, "To be successful in dealing with people from other cultures, managers need knowledge about cultural differences and similarities among countries. They also need to understand the implications of the differences and the skills required to act and decide appropriately and in a culturally sensitive way" (p. 292). Kets de Vries and Florent-Treacy (2002) note that global leadership development means increasing one's adaptability, cultural empathy, acceptance of ambiguity, lack of xenophobia, cultural relativity, awareness of one's own roots and cultural biases, and "as if" quality (p. 307). They go on to note, "An outlook of cultural relativity, excellent relational skills, curiosity, and emotional intelligence distinguish successful global leaders" (p. 304).

Project GLOBE (Global Leadership and Organizational Behavior Effectiveness), an extensive international study of thousands of middle managers, defined culture as "a set of shared values and beliefs" in which the values are "people's aspirations about the way things should be done" and the beliefs are "people's perceptions of how things are done in their countries" (Javidan & House, 2001, p. 293). This study identified nine dimensions of culture that differed from country to country: assertiveness, future orientation, gender differentiation, uncertainty avoidance, power distance (power expected to be shared unequally within the culture), institutional emphasis on collectivism versus individualism, in-group collectivism (membership in small groups and families), performance orientation, and humane orientation (fairness, generosity, caring) (Javidan & House). Some countries seem to be higher than others in different dimensions. For example, people in the United States are thought to be more male-dominated than people in England but less than people in Germany. (See House, Hanges, Javidan, Dorfman, & Gupta, 2004, for the complete report.) As with any attempt to generalize large groups, information in reports such as this should be viewed and used with great caution. That being said, when working with others from different nations, realizing they may differ from you in the dimensions mentioned in this report can help you understand them better and work with them more effectively.

Knowledge about other countries becomes increasingly important as the world becomes more connected. It is also an area in which U.S. students could improve. Rebekah Nathan (2005) is the pen name of an anthropologist who went "undercover" and lived in a residence hall posing as a freshman. As she discovered, "The single biggest complaint international students lodged against U.S. students was, to put it bluntly, our ignorance. As informants described it, by 'ignorance' they meant the misinformation and lack of information that Americans have both about other countries and about themselves" (p. 84).

Presentations

by Ciara Woods

Objectives

- Principles of good presentations

- Planning the presentation

- Writing the presentation

- Constructing slides

- Practising delivery

- Giving the presentation

Giving a presentation is an opportunity to show just how good your communication skills are. It is a chance to show your output to a large audience and is probably one of the fastest routes to success in most companies. This chapter outlines what makes a good presentation and shows you how to go about structuring and writing one. If the thought of giving a presentation makes you break out in a cold sweat, read the sections on dealing with nerves, delivering a presentation and handling questions. There are also sections on presenting as a team, impromptu speaking and attending presentations.

Principles of Good Presentations

It is not always obvious what separates good presentations from bad ones, but you will find that the good ones share a number of common characteristics. They all:

1. Communicate the main point straight away.
2. Are short and to the point.
3. Are easy to understand.
4. Are easy to follow.
5. Have a good layout (and sound good if presented orally).

If you still need convincing, take a look at the two examples below and see which is more efficient at getting the message across and which you would prefer to read.

Example 1

> John,
>
> I have just had a look at the schedule for Project X and there is no way that we are going to meet the deadline. We are already about three weeks behind and it is unlikely that, given the way things are, we can catch up.
>
> As you know, Mary who works on accounts is due to go on maternity leave next week. This will put a further strain on the workload.
>
> Remember when we met last week and you noticed how strained the atmosphere was; team morale is at an all time low. So many people are stressed out and upset that they have so much work to do and not enough time to do it.
>
> For these reasons, I feel that we need another person on the team.
>
> Mark

Example 2

> John,
>
> We need another person on the team. Here are the reasons:
>
> 1. We are 3 weeks behind the deadline for Project X.
> 2. Mary is due to go on maternity leave next week.
> 3. Team morale is low as everyone has too much work to do and too little time.
>
> Mark

A good presentation does not happen by accident. It requires *planning, structuring, writing, editing* and, in the case of oral presentations, *rehearsing*. The remainder of this chapter deals with oral presentations but the approach and procedures for the most part apply equally to written presentations.

Planning the Presentation

A little calm, clear thinking at the outset will save you a great deal of time later. Before you start writing, ask yourself the questions below. The answers to these questions will provide you with the information that will determine the language you use, how deep you need to go into the topic, what you say and how you say it.

Who is your audience?

- What is the general make-up of the audience (number, level, department)?
- What is their relationship with you and with each other?
- What is their current level of knowledge?
- How open are they to change or to new ideas?

Why are you giving the presentation?

- What is the objective of the presentation? (Do you want to argue, defend, educate, entertain, explain, induce action, inform, inspire, motivate, persuade? Or a mixture of these?)
- Were you given a brief?

What is the single most important message of the presentation?

- What is the *one thing* you want everyone in the audience to take home?

Where will the presentation take place?

- Will it be a formal or informal setting?
- Will it be a large or small venue?

When will it be given?

- How much time do you have to prepare it?
- At what time of day will the presentation take place?

How will it be presented?

- Will it be an oral presentation (with slides that will illustrate what you have to say), a written report (a stand-alone document) or a combination?
- It is a good idea to write a detailed document and then simplify it (by removing detail and magnifying the text and graphics) so that you have two documents: one that works as a paper that can be distributed after the presentation and the other as a set of visuals for your presentation.

Structuring the Presentation

At school, you probably learned to structure essays as follows: brief introduction followed by arguments that logically lead to a conclusion. However, most people don't have time to wade through arguments to find out what they need to know; if they don't get the message in the first few minutes, they might never get it.

Minto's Pyramid Principle

Barbara Minto suggests an approach to structuring presentations that she calls 'The Pyramid Principle' from her book of the same name. There are two basic underlying ideas:

1. Every presentation can and should be reduced to a single main message.
   - The pyramid is used as a thinking tool. Start from the bottom of the pyramid and work upwards. The pyramid will have the main message at the top of the pyramid with all the ideas supporting it underneath.
2. The main message should be stated as soon as possible, preferably immediately after a short introduction.
   - The pyramid is used as a communication tool. Start from the top with the main message and work down to the key points and supporting detail.

   Use the structure below (Figure 7-1) to help you write the presentation.

- Start off with an Introduction that sets the context for the presentation and states the main message.
- Support what you have said in the main body of the presentation.
- Finish up with a summary and an outline of the next steps to be taken.

Writing the Presentation

Once you have an objective, a structure and some basic data, you can start to write the presentation. Getting started is often difficult so try the following:

Go somewhere quiet

- Block a period of time during which you can write without any disturbance.

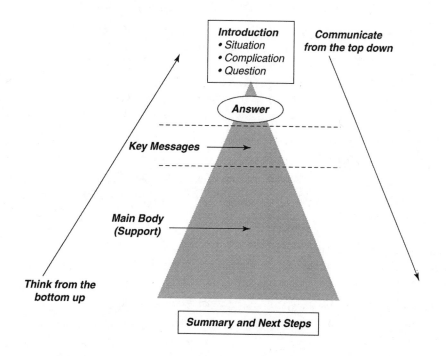

Figure 7-1

A visual interpretation of Minto's Pyramid concept. See Minto, *The Pyramid Principle* for more details.

Write whatever comes into your head

- Let your thoughts flow on to the paper, leaving gaps that can be filled in later if necessary.

Write as you would speak and don't worry about how it sounds

- This stage is about getting your thoughts down, not about style.

Keep reminding yourself what the main message of the presentation is

The Introduction

The introduction is the most important part of the presentation so spend plenty of time thinking it through.

State the situation

- Answer the who, why, what, where and when type questions.
- Ensure the audience starts from the same standpoint as you, the writer.
- Present facts that are indisputable and acceptable to your audience so you immediately establish a rapport.

Outline the complication

- State what happened that changed the situation. This is the complication and it should logically raise a question about what needs to be done.

Pose the question

- It is crucial that the audience is aware of what the presentation is trying to tell them. If they aren't, they won't be able to absorb the answer to your question.
- Make sure you ask the right question, as the main part of the presentation will be spent addressing and hopefully answering the question.

Answer the question (main message of the presentation)

- Make sure your answer is short, relevant and action-oriented. The answer is the single most important message you communicate to the audience.
- The reader should be able to absorb the message in the first 30 seconds.

> **Top Tip**
>
> If you don't ask the right question, you won't get the right answer.

Introduction—Example

(*Situation*) Beta is one of our leading products. It has won numerous awards and has been the leading product in its category for the past five years. (*Complication*) The launch of Gamma last May (by our main competitor) has put pressure on Beta's market share. (*Question*) We were asked to determine how we could maintain our number one position in the marketplace. (*Answer/Resolution*) We have concluded it is possible by:

- Improving availability in rural areas.
- Launching Zeta, a complementary product to Beta.
- Increasing brand awareness among the under-25s sector.

> **Top Tip**
>
> The key to a good presentation is setting things up properly in the introduction.

The Body of the Presentation

Once you have stated the main message of the presentation, you need to let your audience know either why what you said is true or how you are going to achieve what you said. The best way to do this is by logical argument:

Support the main message with some facts (or key messages)

- Try to have about five reasons (or key messages): any less and your support is too weak, any more and your audience will lose track.

Present all of the key messages on one slide

- Then take each of the messages and write a supporting slide (or two) for each one. (See p. 112 on constructing a slide.)

Don't be tempted to overload the slides with information

- It is your job to take all the information and make sense of it for your audience.

Top Tip

The best presentations do not last longer than 20 minutes. Allowing at least one minute per slide, your presentation (including the introduction and conclusion) should have no more than twenty slides.

The Summary and Next Steps

Never forget that no matter how interesting your presentation is or how well you present it, people will be pleased when it comes to an end. The ending, like the introduction, is when the audience's attention is at its highest, so you should spend some time crafting a good one. The end of a presentation has two main functions:

Summarize what has been said already

- Put the main message and major points on a slide. No new information should be included.

Gather momentum for what is to happen next

- Create a slide with a timeline and general outline of what you hope to do over the coming months. The end of a presentation usually signals the start of an initiative, so present this action programme at the end.

Editing the Draft

The first draft is all about the ideas and structure of the document. When you have come up with a draft presentation, it is time to fashion it into an attractive, readable document. When you have finished this, take a break before you start editing. There will be lots of choices to make and making them will not always be easy; you will have to be ruthless. Consider the following:

Top Tip

It is not enough to inform the audience of something; they must be told what they need to do with the information.

Introduction

- Is your opening interesting/engaging?
- Is your purpose defined?

Body

- Is the message clear, relevant and insightful?
- Is the structure logical?

Top Tip

Stop editing when you start making changes that don't justify the time.

- Is the content relevant and compelling?
- Does your tagline state your message and read like a story?
- Are transitions and set-ups smooth?
- Is your language clear and concise?
- Is your tone appropriate?

Ending

- Is the review concise?
- Are the next steps clear?

General

- Is there a balance between words and pictures?
- Are your font, background, graph type and structure consistent?
- Are you using the most appropriate word? Is it spelt correctly?

Constructing Slides

As mentioned at the beginning of the chapter, it is best to write your presentation so that it can work as a stand-alone document (i.e. it has all the information a reader would need) and then go through it and simplify it for presenting. You should end up with two documents: one that works as a paper that can be distributed after the presentation and the other as a set of visuals for your presentation.

A slide should be made up of a message and support for that message. The message takes the form of a 'tagline' or sentence which should appear at the top of the slide. Beneath the tagline, there should be some support for the point being made (see p. 113).

Taglines

The tagline should:

- Be a complete sentence.
- Be informative (i.e. don't just write a title).
- Communicate only one major idea.
- Be relevant.
- Make sense without any graphical support.
- Form a logical part of the story that is being told.

Support

The support should:

- Prove the point made in the tagline.
- Be simple and easy to read (don't fill the slide with information).

- Have immediate impact and be easily understood.
- Be matched to the data it is trying to prove.
- Be consistent with other slides in the presentation in terms of font (type, size and colour), colour scheme, layout and scales.

The biggest mistake that people make when creating slides is that they don't go through that second phase of simplifying the slides and end up presenting slides that are far too detailed. Remember that people are there to listen to you, not to read slides. Keep your slides simple:

Remove unnecessary detail

- Reduce the number of words on the slide.
- Remove all sources and footnotes.

Magnify the text

- The font should be 10 points for handouts and at least 18 points for a slide show presentation.

Magnify the graphics

- Make sure you can see every graphic from the back row of the audience.

Change the background and text colour

- Use a dark background with light text for a slide show presentation.
- Use a light background with dark text for handouts.

Keep colour to a minimum

- Use no more than 3–4 colours throughout the presentation.

> **Top Tip**
>
> Keep slides clean and simple. Add the detail when you speak.

Types of Support

A good visual can really enhance a presentation; a poor or irrelevant one can ruin a presentation, so keep your visuals simple and clear. You can make a

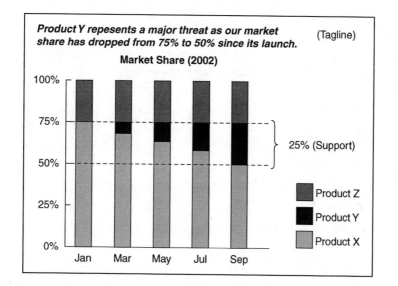

> **Figure 7-2**
>
> Sample Slide

presentation more interesting if you vary the type of support you use. Consider the following:

Bullet points

· Start all the points in the same way (e.g. all with a verb in the same tense).
· Ensure each point conveys a complete thought. Avoid slides that just list words (e.g. Plan, Implement, Assess).
· Never make more than five points.
· Keep slides with bullet points to a minimum; you are there to provide the words.

Tables

· Keep them simple and concise. Only use essential information.
· Confine them to one page.
· Order by columns rather than row, as columns are easier to read.
· Order columns by importance or by size.

Pictures

· Avoid using standard Microsoft clipart. Try to create something original.
· Ensure the pictures keep the tone of the presentation (e.g. don't use cartoons in a serious presentation).

Diagrams

· Make them appropriate; form should never become more important than content.

Videos

· Having video inserts in your presentation gives variety and helps keep your audience focused.
· Make sure all the technology you plan to use is working. The more technology you use, the greater the chance of something going wrong and if something does go wrong, you could end up looking foolish and unprofessional.

Graphs

· Don't insert a graph for the sake of it, as an inappropriate use of a graph adds nothing to a presentation.
· Use the graph that best shows the point you are trying to make. Remember that it is the *message* you want to get across and not the data that determines the type of graph you use.

Top Tip

A few excellent slides will have more impact than lots of mediocre ones.

CHECK LIST Which Type of Chart?	
To show:	
✓ The breakdown of a total:	Use a pie chart.
✓ How things rank:	Use a bar chart.
✓ The relationship between two variables:	Use a paired bar chart.
✓ How something changes overtime:	Use a column or line chart.

Creating Graphs

- Keep graphs simple; there should be just one message per graph.
- Give each graph a meaningful title.
- Use colour for emphasis, not to make them look pretty.
- State the units used (are you dealing with tens, thousands or millions?).
- Source the data.
- Don't clutter the slide with unnecessary notes.

Data Points

- Ensure data groups are discrete (e.g. 1–10, 11–20 *not* 1–10, 10–20).
- Make the data points neat and easy to read (e.g. list them in increasing or decreasing order).
- Emphasize the most important segment or line.
- State the number of data points used underneath the graph (e.g. n = 10).
- Limit the number of data groups to six. (Take the five most important and group the remaining items as 'other'.)

Top Tip

Use the strongest colour for the most important data and position it against the 12 o'clock segment in the case of pie charts and against the baseline in bar and line charts

Practising Delivery

When the presentation is written, there is still much to be done before it should be delivered to an audience. The more formal the situation, the more preparation should be done, but even an informal presentation should be rehearsed before delivery. Try to run through the presentation at least once.

Rehearsing

To give a successful presentation you need to be in control of your material, yourself and your audience. This is a lot to manage, so try to gain mastery of your material and yourself beforehand, and concentrate on the audience on the day.

Record yourself on video (or tape recorder)

- Look for your weak points and work on them but don't become too self-conscious.

CHECK LIST Dos & Don'ts of Delivering a Presentation

Do you:
- ✓ Mumble or talk too fast?
- ✓ Say 'er' and 'um' a lot?
- ✓ Fiddle with your pen or notes?
- ✓ Constantly use certain phrases?
- ✓ Turn your back on or ignore the audience?
- ✓ Pace up and down the floor?

Rehearse out loud

- Time your presentation from beginning to end. It will take longer than you expect.
- Leave a few minutes spare so you don't race through your presentation (e.g. if you have a 20 minute slot, make it a 17 minute presentation).

Rehearse as if it were the real thing

- Run right through without skipping sections and use your notes and aids.
- Rehearse at the venue, if possible.

Rehearse with a friend

- Ask someone who can give you constructive feedback to listen to you.

Rehearse as if everything were to go wrong

- Plan what you would do if you had no visuals, or your time was cut short.

Speaker Notes

If you are confident and feel comfortable with your material, it may be possible to present without using notes, but in general it is a good idea to prepare speaker notes and have them to hand. If you use notes, make sure you don't end up reading them to the audience. Your notes should be:

Short

- Use bullet points, key words, triggers or cues rather than sentences. This way, you will think about what you are saying and sound more convincing.

Easy to follow

- Use extra large type, upper- and lower-case writing, double spacing, high-lighted words, one topic per card and number your cards.
- Keep them loose, never stapled.

Discreet

- You should be able to hold them in one hand only and at arm's length, so you maintain eye contact with the audience.
- Never use A4 sheets.

Tips for Rehearsers

If someone asks you to listen to their presentation:

- Be sensitive: Remember the presentation is tomorrow and this is not the time to undermine the presenter's confidence.
- Be constructive: Don't state a problem without a suggested solution.

- Be objective: Don't make remarks about things that will not make any difference to the message or the audience.
- Be realistic: Help the presenter concentrate on only those changes about which something can be done.

Dealing with Nerves

It is normal, even important, to feel nervous before a presentation. If you don't feel worried at all, you may not be taking the presentation as seriously as you should and are more likely to make mistakes (unless you are a seasoned presenter). Having said that, nerves, if not controlled, can ruin your presentation, so let the adrenalin flow.

Reasons We Feel Nervous and How To Cope

Most of us feel nervous because we are worried that:

We will come across badly

- Remember that no one is perfect; you are allowed to make mistakes. Try to be natural; don't try to be someone that you are not.

We will forget what to say

- Practise, practise, practise until you know your material inside out.
- Write out some speaker notes.

We won't be able to answer people's questions

- Admit it if you don't know the answer. No one expects you to know everything. Say that you will find out the answer and follow up with the person after the presentation.

We won't be able to deal with the unknown when it crops up

- Accept that the unknown probably *will* crop up, so just try to stay calm when it does.

Something will go wrong with the technology

- Make sure you know whom to contact and that you have their contact details.
- Have handouts of the presentation ready, so the show can still go on.

Someone will spot a mistake on the slide

- Don't be embarrassed, just thank them for pointing it out to you and correct what it should say.
- Try to keep mistakes to a minimum by asking someone to proofread your presentation.

Top Tip

Remember that no one is perfect and there is no shame in making a mistake.

Tips for Controlling Nerves

Before the Presentation

Visualize success

- Visit the venue if possible, or get a fax of the room layout. Picture yourself standing at the podium or on the stage, speaking to the audience.

Arrive early

- Make sure you can work the equipment.
- Make sure you have everything that you need.

Talk to the audience

- Try to meet and chat to the audience beforehand, as this will help break down any barriers between you and the audience.

Avoid drinks

- Avoid caffeine or very cold drinks just before speaking, but do try to have something light to eat.
- Go to the toilet before you go on stage.

Breathe

- Do some deep breathing exercises.
- Do some cardiovascular exercise that morning.

Take some time on your own

- Find somewhere quiet where you can spend some time on your own to think through the presentation.

During the Presentation

Compose yourself

- Walk calmly to the stage, organize your notes, look out to the audience and smile. Then take a deep breath and start.

Slow down

- Don't rush the presentation. Think of it as a conversation with the audience.

Think positive

- Keep in the back of your mind how impressed everyone will be if you give a great presentation, not how unimpressed they will be if you don't.

Find a friendly face

- Find support in a friendly face until you are composed.

Preventing Disasters!

Before the event, make sure you have:

1. **The correct version of the presentation.**
    -   Keep version control of the document. Every time you save, save the version (e.g. document name V1 or V2).
    -   Consider putting the version in a small font on the bottom right hand corner of each slide.

2. **Back-ups of the presentation.**
    -   Save the presentation on the hard drive.
    -   Put it on a floppy disk.
    -   Email it to yourself.
    -   Print it out. Photocopy any handouts that you need.

3. **Time with the publishing department (if relevant).**
    -   Book enough time if you are having your presentation professionally published (many companies have in-house departments). Try to book at least a week before you need it. Don't come at the last minute and expect to be facilitated.
    -   Organize overtime help early if you think you will need it.

4. **Checked the room.**
    -   Are there enough chairs?
    -   Can everyone see the screen? Place it at an angle (not directly in front of) your audience. Check if you can read the slides from the back of the room.
    -   Is there a podium? Can it be moved?
    -   Are the lights working?
    -   Is the temperature all right? Make sure it is neither too hot nor too cold.
    -   Is there the appropriate technology (including connections)? Is it working? Run through procedures with the technicians.

5. **Booked all the things you need.**
    -   Organize overhead projectors, flip charts (and markers) or a screen with connections for your laptop if you need them.
    -   Organize beverages for the break, if appropriate.

6. **A list of what you need to take with you.**
    -   Laptop and relevant connections if appropriate.
    -   Material for the presentation (e.g. slides, acetates, videos, models).
    -   Back-up material (e.g. floppy disk, handouts in case of technical failure).
    -   Details of people you can contact if you have other requirements on the day (e.g. who can change the room temperature, get more chairs or sort out technical difficulties).

> **Top Tip**
>
> Never leave copying until the last minute as invariably photocopiers get jammed, run out of paper or take ages to warm up.

Giving the Presentation

Never forget that the people in the audience probably dislike having to be there, even more than you dislike having to present. When people come to a presentation, they come *prepared* to listen. Your aim, as the presenter is to make them *want* to listen. You have succeeded if you have grabbed and held the audience's attention and they have understood everything you said.

Presentation Sequence

A good presentation, like a good story, must have a definite beginning, middle and end. A good story must also be simple, to the point and easy to remember. The best way to achieve this is through repetition:

1. Tell them what you are going to tell them (Introduction).
2. Tell them (Key messages and supporting data).
3. Tell them what you've told them (Conclusion).

The Opening

A strong opening is crucial for a successful presentation. If you don't create an impact and arrest the audience's attention from the word go, you will not be given a second chance. You need to connect with your audience from the start. Try to:

Grab the audience's attention

- Start the presentation with a quotation, story, fact or question.
- Be as enthusiastic as you want your audience to be.

Establish yourself as a credible and authoritative figure

- Say who you are and why you are speaking on this topic.

Address the audience directly

- Thank everyone for coming.
- Make it clear what participation you expect.
- Work to decrease the psychological divide that tends to exist between speaker and audience (e.g. never turn your back to the audience, avoid using 'I' and always use 'we' rather than 'you').

Outline the presentation format

- State what you are going to talk about and why.
- State when you will take questions.
- State if you will be handing out copies of the presentation.

Let people know the timing

- State how long the presentation will be and if there will be breaks.

The Body of the Presentation

During the body of the presentation you must lead the audience through a clear and logical argument. Make sure you:

Tell a logical story

- Present the points in the same sequence as outlined in your opening.
- Point out what each slide was designed to show (never put up a slide and take it down without explaining it).
- Relate each section to the big picture.
- Make it obvious when you are moving from one section to the next.

Keep your language simple

- Keep your sentences short and avoid idioms, slang or sarcasm, especially if you have an international audience.

Correct yourself if you make a mistake and move on

- Don't panic if you make a mistake, it happens to everyone at some time.

Watch the audience's reaction

- Keep an eye on your audience's reaction and adjust your presentation accordingly (e.g. if they look bored, change your tone or ask a question; if they look confused, restate what you have said in more simple terms).
- Give the audience time to digest the information on each slide before commenting on it.

Keep an eye on time to make sure you are on track

- Cut out the less important things if you are running out of time.
- Don't be afraid to finish early if you are getting through it sooner than planned.

Bring your presentation alive

- Bring the presentation alive through your voice and body language; people have come to hear you, not to read slides.

Voice

Volume

- Speak loudly enough to allow people in the back row hear you.
- Increase and decrease the volume of your voice to emphasize key points.
- Don't tail off towards the end of a point.

Pitch

- Avoid sounding monotonous by varying the pitch of your voice.
- Use downward inflections. They sound more confident and persuasive than upward inflections.

Pace

- Take care to speak more slowly than you would in an everyday context. Nerves often make people ramble, so make a conscious effort to slow down and speak clearly and distinctly.

Pause

- Don't be afraid of silence—the pause is an incredibly powerful technique.
- A good pause should be longer than you think is necessary.

Body Language

Hands

- Keep your hands loosely by your sides.
- Don't cross your arms, put them behind your back, in your pockets, through your hair or on your hips.
- Don't fidget. Leave pens down unless you need to write something.

Eyes

- Look people in the eye; do not stare through them.
- Don't focus on just one person; look at several people, spending no longer than a few seconds on each.
- Look for a friendly face if the audience seems hostile.

Face

- Keep your head up. Smile and look happy to be there.

Movement

- Stand tall with equal weight on each foot. Never shift from foot to foot.
- Make the space around you your own and use it to narrow the psychological distance between you and the audience.
- Make any movement confident and deliberate.
- Be natural and let your personality come through. Don't force yourself to be too still and don't pace up and down.

The Ending of the Presentation

Make it obvious that you have reached the end of your presentation.

- Round off the talk with a summary of what you have already said.
- Draw some concrete conclusions or recommendations and suggest next steps.
- End on a high note.
- Thank the audience for listening and then open the floor to questions (you could take questions during the presentation but it can be distracting).

Answering Questions

Open up the question session to everyone without exception and show everyone equal respect. Remember, there is no such thing as a stupid question. Plant someone in the audience with a question or have some questions up your sleeve in case no one asks one. This gives people time to compose a question of their own. When you are asked a question:

1. **Listen to the question.**
   - Give your full attention to the questioner.
   - Note down some points if the question is long or complex.
   - Do not start to answer until you are sure that the speaker has finished.

2. **Make sure you have understood the question before answering.**
   - Thank the questioner for their 'interesting' or 'important' question.
   - Paraphrase to ensure you have understood correctly and that everyone is aware of what the question is.

3. **Pause to think about the answer.**
   - Let the questioner know you are considering your answer.

4. **Answer.**
   - Look at the whole group when answering, not just at the questioner.
   - Relate the question back to the main message of your presentation.
   - Give a concise answer at a level appropriate to your audience. If a longer explanation is required, offer to speak to the questioner after the session.
   - Make sure that the questioner is satisfied with your response.

Dealing with Difficult Questions

Questions can often catch us out and make us feel ill at ease. It is imperative that you don't let your emotions take over. If this happens and you feel yourself getting angry or upset, take a moment to control how you feel before answering. You can buy yourself time by calmly asking the questioner to elaborate or refine their question.

If you can't answer the question:

- If you don't know the answer to a question admit it, but offer to find out the answer afterwards and do keep your promise.

If a question is asked before you deal with the topic:

- Tell the questioner that you will be dealing with their point later and ask if they would mind waiting until then. It is very impressive if you remember to turn to the relevant person with the answer when you reach the appropriate topic.

If the question is awkward or irrelevant:

- Remain cool, calm and collected and ask if you could discuss it during the break (as time won't allow an appropriate answer).

Top Tip

Don't think of it as you versus them; the audience is not the enemy.

Top Tip

When you start running out of time, signal that the next question will be the last. After you answer it, thank everyone for coming.

Top Tip

Anticipate the most obvious questions [think about who will be present and what departments they are from— people tend to ask questions related to their own specific field] and prepare responses, including back-up material, if appropriate.

Top Tip

If someone is giving a speech when asking a question, end it diplomatically

If the question is aggressive or hostile:

- Show understanding for what the questioner is saying and try to find common ground.
- Depersonalize the question by either asking for an example or by rewording it in non-emotional language.
- Answer in a calm and objective way. Never raise your voice and argue or debate.
- Give a succinct answer and move on.

Presenting as a Team

There may be occasions when you have to present as a team. If the occasion arises, keep the following in mind:

Have clearly defined roles

- Look and act like a team.
- Make sure everyone knows their role.
- Explain the different roles and why people are presenting different sections. If someone isn't presenting, make sure there is a reason for them to be there.

Create a seamless presentation

- Give someone the responsibility of making sure that the slides are consistently formatted.
- Make a smooth handover to the next speaker. Summarize your points and introduce the speaker and topic of the next section, at the end of your section. Never use clichés like 'So over to you John' or 'So, without further ado—Mary—go for it!'

Refer, support and repeat the central message

- Keep the 'argument' coherent, with each section logically moving on from the previous one and strengthening the overall message.
- Repeat your message. It is better to have each of the speakers talk on different aspects of the same theme than on separate themes.
- Support each other's arguments by referring back to them (e.g. 'As Kate said . . .' or 'Let me add to what Will has told you'). Avoid saying things like 'I shan't bore you by repeating what Claire was saying'.

Look interested in what is being said

- When you are waiting to present or have finished presenting, give your full attention to the person speaking, even though you may know their speech off by heart. Never stare into the audience or shuffle through your notes.

Top Tip

One theme repeated three times will have far more impact than three separate themes.

Impromptu Speaking

A great impromptu speaker always sounds prepared. This may sound like a contradiction in terms but it can be achieved if you:

Know what you would say before you are asked

- Jot down (or imagine) what points you would make, if you were asked to speak.

Take your time

- Don't say the first thing that comes into your head. Decide what point you want to make before you say anything; silence is less embarrassing than rambling.

Make eye contact

- Speak *to*, not *at* the people in the room.

Keep it brief and to the point

- Make about three points, listing all of them first and then giving a quick summary on each one.
- Think of it as a mini-presentation that should be structured and well delivered.

Top Tip

Collect examples, short anecdotes and quotations in a notebook and memorize them as it is impressive and professional looking if you can start an impromptu speech with a relevant one.

Attending Presentations

When you start out in your career, you will probably attend more presentations than you give. There are certain things you should and should not do when invited to one.

CHECK LIST	Dos & Don'ts
✓ Decide if it's relevant to attend.	✗ Don't start a conversation or mutter asides with the people beside you.
✓ Confirm your attendance.	✗ Don't show boredom [e.g. sigh or yawn loudly].
✓ Give your full attention to the speaker.	✗ Don't ask awkward, irrelevant, aggressive or hostile questions.
✓ Be able to summarize the presentation (speakers, main points, the outcome).	✗ Don't air opinions later to selected colleagues that you were too cowardly to bring into open discussion.
✓ Sit near a door if you have to leave early.	

Reading Graphs

Don't just accept everything you see at face value, especially when you are shown graphs. Everyone likes to show things in their best light, but that often means that certain truths are hidden. Make sure you:

Check the scale for distortions. Has it been:

- Expanded to make something look bigger?
- Contracted to make something look smaller?
- Inverted to make a fall look like a rise?

Consider what may have been left out

- Two points on a line showing a rise might cover up a steep fall in between.
- What happened before the start of the graph?

Check values for appropriateness

- Have two data sets been converted to base 100? (i.e. making the first number equal 100 and changing the rest accordingly). If so, it can be very misleading as both sets of data converge on the base.

Top Tip

Don't be fooled by graphs. Ask yourself:

- What exactly is being graphed?
- What are the units on the axes?
- What could the graph be hiding?

Why We Hate PowerPoints—and How to Fix Them

By Nancy Duarte, Special to CNN

Story Highlights

- Army officer fired after publishing essay complaining about useless PowerPoints
- Nancy Duarte says bad presentations obscure or conceal key points
- She says successful presentations don't win because of a wealth of data
- Duarte: What makes a PowerPoint work is great storytelling

Editor's note: *Nancy Duarte is the author of "Resonate: Present Visual Stories that Transform Audiences." She is CEO of Duarte Design, a presentation design firm based in Mountain View, California, that worked with Al Gore on the presentation featured in "An Inconvenient Truth" and whose clients include Cisco, Facebook, Google, TED and the World Bank.*

(CNN)—A few weeks ago Col. Lawrence Sellin, a Special Forces officer stationed in Afghanistan, fell victim to a particularly modern hazard of war: PowerPoint fatigue.

Col. Sellin was fired from his post at NATO's International Security Assistance Force after he wrote an essay for the UPI wire service in which he voiced his frustration about PowerPoint-obsessed officers who spend more time worrying about font size and bullet points than actual bullets.

Col. Sellin's was just the latest in a series of complaints about the military use of slide presentations—you may recall public ridicule of the famously incomprehensible "spaghetti slide," and a recent *New York Times* article, that cited other officers just as frustrated with the emergence of the military bureaucracy's "PowerPoint rangers."

But PowerPoint isn't inherently bad—just misunderstood. And bad PowerPoint presentations aren't just a concern of the military. We've all sat through presentations—or suffered or even dozed through them. The truth is, most are poorly constructed and instantly forgettable.

Why does this matter? Because presentations decide elections, military strategies and multibillion-dollar business deals; they educate our children and they spread the ideas that shape society's most important goals and directives.

Ultimately, a presentation succeeds or falls on the strength of its message and how well it's told. And those elements have nothing to do with the brand of the software package involved in its production. You know instantly when you're watching a great presenter at work—you may even own the ShamWow to prove it.

Sometimes, presenters try to punch up weak content with stunts. I remember one speaker who rode onto the stage on a motorcycle—and promptly lost control and crashed. (He was okay.) Another presenter rappelled down to the stage like a mountain climber. I remember the stunts, but not the messages.

Poor presentations can have disastrous consequences. Edward Tufte, perhaps the most important writer on the display of information, demonstrated how the disintegration of the space shuttle Columbia in 2003 might have been averted by a more objective presentation of the damage inflicted on Columbia's wing by a piece of foam debris during takeoff.

As it was, Tufte wrote in his article, "PowerPoint Does Rocket Science: Assessing the Quality and Credibility of Technical Reports," NASA officials came away from PowerPoint-driven briefings by Boeing engineers with an overly optimistic view of the situation, in part as a result of hard-to-understand slides overloaded with bullet points. In other words, a bad presentation may have caused that disaster, and a good one might have prevented it.

Of course, we can't be naive: a persuasive presentation isn't necessarily a good presentation. In 2001, Enron Corp. executives Ken Lay, Jeff Skilling and Richard Causey presented PowerPoint slides at an employee meeting that winningly depicted the company's robust health and the bright future of its projected earnings. By the end of that year the company was worthless. Eventually, the U.S. Department of Justice charged those executives with 10 counts of a variety of crimes—based on their presentations.

Meanwhile, the Enron scandal may have been preventable by the right presentation. In 1999, a presentation by the Arthur Andersen accounting firm feebly warned the Enron Board of Director's audit committee of the company's sketchy accounting. Had that presentation sounded a bold warning, the audit committee might have been able to save the company. For that matter, it might have saved Andersen, which did not recover from its role in Enron's dealings.

Unfortunately, the development of presentations is a skill that is rarely taught and for which few sources of best practices exist. Bad presentations kill ideas, waste money and impede progress. Great ones illuminate, persuade, generate consensus and spark action.

How do you create a great presentation? I've been in the business for 20 years, but until recently even I couldn't define the deep structures and elements of truly superior presentations.

My research into this question led me in unexpected directions. The answers I found had nothing to do with technology or the internet; they were revealed in screenwriting, Greek and Shakespearean drama, mythology and literature.

Great presenters employ the basic narrative techniques used throughout history to connect with audiences and move them to action and new understanding.

The presentations that work are not the ones with the most data or the most elaborate charts and graphs; the winners are those with the most compelling and convincing narratives.

We're a distracted, multi-tasking society. So presentations need to lure and re-lure an audience simply to keep their attention. Audiences are looking at the clock or fiddling with their handheld devices throughout a presentation. You don't connect with your audience by throwing information at them—you do it by taking them on a journey toward your perspective.

Whether you're a CEO, a salesperson, a general or a biochemist, you must understand how to connect with an audience, how to construct a powerful narrative argument, and how to visually display information for maximum audience comprehension.

I read recently that our nation is suffering a crisis of literacy, with only 35% percent of high school seniors able to read proficiently. Yes, you read that correctly (assuming you're not part of the 65% of high school seniors.) But literacy really means the ability to communicate effectively. For professionals and citizens in every strata of society, true literacy now includes the ability to communicate effectively through presentations.

The stakes could not be higher for our country. If corporate executives communicate poorly, businesses and the economy suffer, and jobs are lost. If teachers communicate poorly, our children don't learn and advance. If generals communicate poorly, our troops and their missions are put at risk. These are dangers we cannot ignore.

The opinions expressed in this commentary are solely those of Nancy Duarte.

Find this article at:

http://www.cnn.com/2010/OPINION/10/15/duarte.powerpoint.fatigue/index.html?hpt=T2

Résumé Package

by Lydia E. Anderson and Sandra B. Bolt

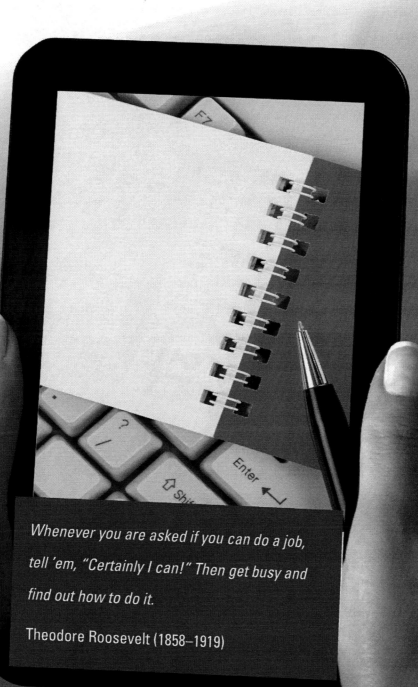

> *Whenever you are asked if you can do a job, tell 'em, "Certainly I can!" Then get busy and find out how to do it.*
>
> Theodore Roosevelt (1858–1919)

Objectives

- Identify the steps for building a résumé package
- Write a career objective or personal profile
- Distinguish between a *functional résumé* and a *chronological résumé*
- Identify personal *soft skills, job-specific skills,* and *transferable skills*
- Create a winning *résumé*
- Write a *cover letter*

How-Do-You-Rate

	Test your resume expertise	True	False
1.	Paper résumés are not necessary in today's electronic age.	☐	☐
2.	Career objectives are used on all resumes.	☐	☐
3.	Unique skills such as being bilingual or serving in the military can lead to discrimination and should not be listed on a formal résumé.	☐	☐
4.	Using a word-processing résumé template is best when creating a résumé.	☐	☐
5.	If I have a job gap on my résumé it is acceptable to make up a job to fill in the gap.	☐	☐

If you answered "true" to at least two questions, use the information and tools in this chapter to improve your chances of creating and utilizing a winning résumé.

Building Your Résumé Package

Before an employer meets you, they first view your résumé package. A résumé package includes a résumé and a cover letter. Your résumé needs accents package needs to efficiently and effectively sell your skills and communicate how your attributes are unique compared to those of all the other candidates vying for your target job. A **résumé** is a formal written profile that presents a person's knowledge, skills, and abilities to potential employers. Your résumé is an important job search tool that should be continually updated throughout your career. You may not be planning to find a new job or get promoted today, but a time will come when a current résumé is needed. Do not wait until that time to create or update your résumé. As you increase your job skills and accomplishments, add these new skills and experiences to your résumé.

When you begin to create your résumé, you will quickly discover that there are various types of résumés and résumé formats. You may also receive conflicting advice as to how the perfect résumé should look and what it should include. The appropriate type of résumé used depends upon your work experience. A well-written résumé makes it easy for potential employers to quickly and easily identify your skills and work experience.

This chapter will present the tools for creating a professional résumé and cover letter. As you go through the process of constructing your résumé package, make every word, the visual presentation, and the information sell your skills and career accomplishments. There are five steps toward building a winning résumé:

- *Step One:* Career Objective/Personal Profile
- *Step Two:* Gathering Information

- *Step Three:* Proper Layout
- *Step Four:* Skills, Accomplishments, and Experience
- *Step Five:* The Final Résumé

Step One: Career Objective/Personal Profile

The first step in developing a winning résumé is to write a career objective or personal profile. A career objective is a statement that presents your key skills in a brief statement for individuals with little or no work experience. A personal profile is used for individuals with more extensive career experience. Create a career objective or personal profile. Use your career objective or personal profile as the foundation for your résumé. Make your career objective or personal profile specific to the job for which you are applying.

Exercise 8-1   Your Career Objective or Personal Profile

Write a career objective or personal profile.

_____

_____

_____

_____

Step Two: Gathering Information

The second step in building a résumé is to create a draft document with key headings. This step involves collecting and merging all relevant information into one document. Begin identifying and listing the following information into an electronic document:

1. *Education.* List schools, dates, degrees, certificates, credentials, GPA, licenses, and other relevant education information, including military experience.
2. *Skills.* List all skills you possess.
3. *Employment.* Starting with the most recent job, list the employer, dates of employment (month and year), job title, and responsibilities.
4. *Languages.* List all foreign languages, fluency levels, and if you can read, speak, and/or write the foreign language.
5. *Honors and Awards.* List any honors and awards you have received at school, work, or from the community.
6. *Professional/Community Involvement.* List volunteer work and community service projects. Include any leadership role you took in these activities.

Note that when compiling information to include in your résumé, there is no personal information listed. Personal information including birth date, marital/child status, ethnicity, or religion should not be included on a résumé. It is also inappropriate to list hobbies or include photographs. There are laws that protect employees from discrimination in hiring and advancement in the workplace, and employers should not be aware of personal information unless it is relevant to the job for which you are applying. Older job seekers should not list the date of graduation on a résumé as it could be used for age discrimination.

Exercise 8-2   Gather Information

Complete the following table:

Education (list most recent first)

School Name	City, State	Dates	Degree, Certificate, Credential, Licenses

Skills

Employment (list most recent first)

Employer	Employment Dates	Job Title	Duties

Exercise 8-2   Gather Information (continued)

Languages	Fluency (Read, Write, and/or Speak)

Honors and Awards	Dates	Place

Professional/Community Involvement		

Step Three: Proper Layout

The third step in developing a successful résumé is to identify and arrange your information in the proper résumé layout. If you are at the start of your career and/or do not have extensive work experience, create a résumé using the **functional résumé layout.** This layout is used to emphasize relevant skills when you lack related work experience. A functional résumé focuses on skills and education. When writing a functional résumé, list your career objective, relevant skills, and education before any work experience. Include only your high school in the education section if you are using a functional layout and have not yet graduated from college. Most functional résumés are only one page in length. Refer to Figure 8-1 for the functional résumé layout, and see Figures 8-2 and 8-3 for examples of a functional résumé with and without career-related work experience.

Functional Résumé Layout, see Figure 8-1 on page 140

Those with extensive career experience should use a **chronological résumé layout.** In the chronological layout, note that the career objective is replaced with a personal profile. General skills emphasized in a personal profile are key skill sets. These skill sets will be used as subheadings in the professional experience section on a chronological résumé. The chronological layout presents related work experience, skills, and significant accomplishments under each respective skill set subheading. When writing a personal profile, include

Functional Résumé Example with Minimal Career Work Experience, see Figure 8-2 on page 142

Functional Résumé Example without Career Work Experience, see Figure 8-3 on page 143

Talk It Out

Which résumé layout is best for your situation? Why?

Chronological Résumé Layout, see Figure 8-4 on page 144

Chronological Résumé Example with Degree, see Figure 8-5 on pages 145–146

Chronological Résumé Example with No Degree, see Figure 8-6 on page 146

key general skills and key qualities desired by your target employer. Specific skills will be detailed under each respective professional experience subheading. Share major accomplishments and responsibilities from each position. Include important activities you have accomplished in your job. If necessary, add a second page to your résumé. A chronological layout best highlights, communicates, and sells specific job skills and work accomplishments. Refer to Figure 8-4 for the chronological résumé layout, and see Figures 8-5 and 8-6 for examples of chronological résumés.

For both functional and chronological résumé layouts, present employment history and education in reverse time order (most recent job first). When listing work history, bold your job title, not the place of employment. When listing dates of employment, use only month and year. Be consistent in how dates are listed on the résumé.

When you have determined which résumé layout is best for your current situation, electronically arrange the information you have compiled into the correct résumé layout. Avoid résumé templates. Résumé templates can be difficult to update, modify, and personalize.

Step Four: Skills, Accomplishments, and Experience

Once you have electronically arranged your information into the correct layout, it is time to move to the fourth step in developing your résumé. This involves detailing the information listed in your skills, work experience, and professional accomplishments. Work experience includes learned skills, job duties, and accomplishments. Professional accomplishments communicate specific activities you achieved beyond your job duties. Whenever possible, quantify your skills, responsibilities, and professional accomplishments. Do not assume the reader will know what you have done. As you insert professional accomplishments and responsibilities into your electronic file, include both job-specific skills and transferable skills. **Job-specific skills** are those that are directly related to a specific job or industry. If you were to change careers, job-specific skills would probably not be useful. For example, if you are a medical billing clerk who knows how to use a specific software program such as Medical Manager, you will not need to use this skill if you become a preschool teacher.

Transferable skills are skills that are transferred from one job to the next. If you change careers, you will still be able to use (transfer) these skills in any job. For example, if you are a medical billing clerk, you may have learned customer service skills from consistent contact with patients and must practice being positive when dealing with customers. If you become a preschool teacher, the customer service skill of being positive is transferable to the children in your classroom. Employers need employees with job-specific skills and transferable skills, so list both types on your résumé. The term **soft skills** refers to the people skills necessary when working with others in the workplace. Employers want employees that are reliable, team players, good communicators, and able to get along well with others.

When listing work experience on your résumé, include the job title, company name, city, and state where the company is located, and the duties of the position. When listing job duties, be specific with common workplace skills, such as computer skills. The term computer skills can be too general and typically includes many different areas: networking, programming, applications, data processing, and/or repair. An employer needs to know what specific computer skills you possess. For example, inform the employer of your computer skill level (e.g., basic, intermediate, or advanced) with a specific software. When listing your skills, first list the skills relevant to your target job. If you are bilingual include this information in your résumé. Let the employer know what second language you read, write, or speak.

Résumés do not normally contain complete sentences. They contain statements that sell your skills, qualifications, and work experience. Except for the career objective on a functional résumé, the words "I" and "my" should not appear.

Exercise 8-3 Detail Your Skills

List as many job-specific and transferable skills as possible. If you do not have any job-specific skills, list the job skills you will have after finishing your schooling.

Job-Specific Skills (Related to Your Career Job)	Transferable Skills (Can Be Used in Any Job)
1.	1.
2.	2.
3.	3.
4.	4.
5.	5.

When applying for a specific position, identify the key knowledge, skills, and abilities the employer desires. General information regarding a specific position will be listed in the job announcement. If possible, secure a copy of the job description. If this is not possible, use the target job information or conduct an occupational quick search on the O*Net database. This database of occupational information was developed for the U.S. Department of Labor and provides key information by job title. Match the key knowledge, skills, and abilities required for your target job with the knowledge, skills, and abilities you possess. Then emphasize this information on your résumé.

Organize your skills and work experience by first listing the key skills required for your target job. When communicating your skills, experience, and accomplishments, write with energy. Use action verbs, also referred to as **power words.** Power words are action verbs that describe your accomplishments in a lively and specific way. For example, instead of stating "started a new accounts receivable system," use "developed a new accounts receivable system that reduced turnaround time by 20 percent." Power words are listed in Table 8-1 and Table 8-2.

Exercise 8-4   Accomplishments

Refer back to the accomplishments worksheet you completed in Exercise 8-1. Review these accomplishments and turn them into powerful action statements. Quantify whenever possible.

Choose Your Top Five Accomplishments from Exercise 8-1	Change to Powerful Action Statements
1.	
2.	
3.	
4.	
5.	

Table 8-1   Skills Power Words

Sample Power Statements for Skills

- Ideal oral and written communications skills

- Understanding of office practices and procedures; ability to operate fax machine, copy machine, and ten-key machine; ability to enter data; ability to effectively interpret policies and procedures; work well under the pressure of deadlines; establish and maintain a positive working relationship with others; ability to communicate

- Accurate typing skills at _____ wpm

- Experienced with Microsoft Office, including Word, Excel, Access, PowerPoint, and Outlook

- Excellent English grammar, spelling, and punctuation skills

- Accurately proofread and edit documents

- Strong attention to detail

- Accurately follow oral and written instructions

- Excellent attendance and punctuality record

- Maintain confidentiality

- Positive attitude, motivated, and organized

Step Five: Complete the Résumé

Prior to finalizing your résumé, ensure that you have added all information identified in steps one through four to your electronic document. As you finalize your résumé, check for information that too frequently is forgotten or not presented appropriately. This is the fifth step in finalizing the information

Table 8-2   Experience Power Words

Sample Power Statement for Work Experience

- Prepared reports and other materials requiring independent achievement

- Enjoy working in a flexible team situation

- Established and maintained positive and effective working relationships

- Planned, scheduled, and performed a variety of clerical work

- Maintained office equipment and supplies

- Proofread forms and materials for completeness and accuracy according to regulations and procedures

- Processed and prepared materials for pamphlets, bulletins, brochures, announcements, handbooks, forms, and curriculum materials

- Provided training of temporary or new employees

- Maintained department files and records

- Demonstrated ability to receive incoming calls and route them efficiently

- Processed purchase requisitions, ordered and distributed supplies, and maintained inventory control

- Responsibly planned and conducted meetings

on your résumé. The top of your résumé is called the **information heading.** An information heading contains relevant contact information including name, mailing address, city, state, ZIP code, contact phone, and e-mail address. Include your complete and formal name, including a middle initial if you have one. When listing your e-mail address, remove the hyperlink so the print color is consistent. If your current e-mail address is unprofessional, secure an address that is professional. Include only one contact phone number. Whatever number is listed should be active and have a professional voice-mail message. Check the spelling and numbers for accuracy. Spell out the names of streets. If you use abbreviations, check for appropriate format, capitalization, and punctuation.

Immediately after your information heading is the career objective or personal profile created in step one. Review this opening statement to ensure it introduces the reader to who you are and motivates him or her to learn more about your specific knowledge, skills, abilities, and key accomplishments.

In step three, you determined whether a functional or chronological résumé layout was appropriate for your situation. Review the respective layout for proper order and refer to the sample résumés. Confirm that your experience and education are listed chronologically (most recent first). Keep your résumé consistent in its setup, including all periods or no periods at the end of each line, line spacing, alignment of dates, date format, bold/italics, upper- and lowercase words, and underlines. Be consistent with word endings and the use of tense in each section (e.g., *-ing* and *-ed*). Also be consistent with the use of the postal abbreviation for your state (e.g., the state is *CA*, not *Ca.*, not *Ca,* not *C.A*). When your draft résumé is complete, spell-check and proofread the document to ensure it is free of typographical errors and inconsistencies.

As for proper résumé layout and design, underlines, bold, and italic print are acceptable for emphasis but should not be overdone. Do not use bullets throughout your résumé; use bullets only to emphasize key skills. Use easy-to-read fonts and sizes. Times New Roman or Arial are most common. Apart from your name on the information heading of your résumé, do not use more than two different font sizes, preferably 12 to 14 points. Do not use different color fonts, highlights, or graphics on your résumé; use only black ink. It is not appropriate to include personal information such as a photograph of yourself, your birth date, marital status, Social Security number, or hobbies. It is also no longer appropriate to state, "References Available Upon Request" at the close of your résumé. Professional references should be on a separate sheet and provided only when requested. Refer to Figure 8-11 for proper format for a professional reference list.

Tailored Package, See
Figure 8-11 on
page 151

Check to ensure your résumé is presented professionally, is free of errors, and does not contain unnecessary or inappropriate information. Print the résumé in black ink on 8½ × 11–inch, letter-sized paper. Laser print is ideal. Double-sided résumés are not appropriate. If your résumé is more than one page, place your name at the top of each page after page one. Proper résumé paper is cotton-fiber, 24-pound white (not bond or card stock) paper of good quality. Colored paper, especially if dark, is both difficult to read and does not photocopy well. Do not use fancy paper stocks or binders. Do not staple your résumé or other job search documents. Since résumés are frequently photo-copied, stapled résumés and other job search documents may be torn in the process.

When you have completed your résumé and believe it is ready for distribution, have several individuals whom you trust review it for clarity, consistency, punctuation, grammar, typographical errors, and other potential mistakes. Remember that complete sentences are not necessary and, with the exception of your career objective, the words "I" or "my" should not be used. Your résumé must create a positive, professional visual image and be easy to read.

Sharing Your Résumé

As you begin to share your completed résumé with both potential employers and members of your professional network, you may have the option of presenting your résumé on résumé paper (traditional hard copy) or electronically (online) as an attachment. Résumés printed on résumé paper are designed to be used for face-to-face job searches. Regardless of which method you choose, the first step is to perfect your traditional (hard-copy) résumé, as this document contains key information you will need to share with all potential employers. When converting a traditional (hard-copy) résumé into an online version, consider content. When forwarding a résumé to an employer or posting your résumé online, such as on a job board, consider key words that reflect your target job. When employers and job boards receive résumés, the résumés are commonly dropped into a database or résumé tracking system that allow recruiters to search for potential applicants based on key words and phrases

Exercise 8-5 Check for Inconsistencies

Circle the fifteen inconsistency errors on the following résumé.

1100 EAST FAVOR AVENUE • POSTVILLE, PA 16722
PHONE (555) 698-2222 • E-MAIL AERIE@PBCC.COM

AMANDA J. ERIE

OBJECTIVE

Seeking a position as an Administrative Assistant where I can utilize my office skills

SUMMARY OF QUALIFICATIONS

- Computer software skills include Microsoft Word, Excel, Outlook, Access, and PowerPoint
- Knowledge of Multi-line telephone system, filing, data entry, formatting of documents and reports, and operation of office equipment.
- Excellent interpersonal skills and polished office etiquette.
- written and oral communication skills
- Typing skills at 50 WPM
- Bilingual in English/Spanish (speaking)

EDUCATION

Reese Community College, Postville, PA Currently pursuing AA Degree in Office Occupations.

Calvin Institute of Technology, Cambridge, OH Office Technology Certificate Spring 2010

WORK AND VOLUNTEER EXPERIENCE

01/11 – Present   *Rigal Entertainment Group*   Postville, CA
Usher – Responsible for ensuring payment of services. Answer customer inquiries. Collect and count ticket stubs.

11/07 – 02/09   Lablaws   Cambridge, OH
Cashier – Operated cash register, stocking, assisting customers

01/07 – 04/07   Jolene's Diner   Cambridge, OH
Server – Provided customer service by waiting tables, cleaned, and operated cash register

that match the position they are trying to fill. Sometimes, when posting an online résumé, you may be required to cut and paste sections from your traditionally formatted résumé. During this process, you may lose the formatting. Do not worry. Visual appeal is not an issue for this process and formatting does not matter. You are merely dropping your information into a database. Your focus should be on utilizing key words and phrases that sell your skills and quantify your accomplishments.

The second consideration when converting a traditional résumé to an online version is sending it as an attachment while preserving formatting. If you are sending your résumé electronically as an attachment, it is best to send it either as a Microsoft (MS) Word file or as a portable document file (.pdf). Doing so ensures that the résumé layout is properly maintained through the file transfer. Sending your résumé as a .pdf file also ensures that those who do not use the same word processing software as you are able to read the file.

Most colleges and career centers now have electronic job boards that allow students to upload their résumés for recruiters and employers to view. There are also many niche job boards specific to industries. Another popular means of sharing an electronic résumé is through social media sites. Just be certain that you are posting your information on valid business sites and not personal sites. As with a traditional job search, keep track of and monitor all activity with your online search.

When posting your résumé online, always date your resume and update it every two to three months. Most employers won't view online résumés that are more than six months old. Guard your personal information by posting your résumé only on reputable job search sites. Just as with a hard-copy résumé, protect your identity and do not include personal information of any kind, including photographs, marital status, birth dates, or your Social Security number.

In some instances employers, will request that an **electronic formatted résumé** be submitted. Electronic formatted résumés are résumés that are submitted in American Standard Code for Information Interchange (ASCII) format. Once the employer receives your electronic formatted résumé, the résumé is added to a specialized database/software that routinely scans résumés based on key words (qualifications/skills) for specific jobs. The résumé is used to match key words contained in your résumé with specific jobs. Therefore, on this type of résumé, list as many key words as possible related to your target job. For electronic formatted résumés, visual appeal is not an issue. Electronic formatted résumés use Times New Roman font size 10 to 14. An electronic formatted résumé should be left-justified. Avoid tabs and centering. Headings should be in all capital letters. Hard returns must be used instead of word wrap. Avoid bold, italics, underlines, graphics, percent signs, and foreign characters. Also avoid boxes, horizontal and vertical lines, solid/hollow bullets, and table and column formatting.

Content for electronic formatted résumés include having your name at the top of the page on its own line. Standard address formatting (as when addressing a letter) should be used. Use key words specific to your desired job category and/or when communicating your knowledge, skills, and abilities. Work experience dates should have beginning and ending dates on the same line. Use asterisks or dashes (no bullets or boxes of any kind) and list each telephone number on its own line (no parentheses around area codes). Date your electronic résumé. Just as with hard-copy résumés, do not include personal information of any kind, including photographs, marital status, birth dates, or your Social Security number. See Figure 8-7 for an example of an electronic formatted résumé.

Electronic Résumé Example, see Figure 8-7 on page 147

Cover Letters

A **cover letter** is often the first impression a potential employer will have of you. It serves as an introduction to your résumé. Employers use cover letters as screening tools.

When writing a cover letter, use a friendly but professional tone. Use complete sentences and proper grammar. When tailoring your cover letter, include information about the target company that communicates to the employer you have conducted research on the company. In a cover letter, communicate how your key skills, experience, and accomplishments can meet the employer's needs. This is accomplished by identifying the skills and qualifications the target employer is requesting in the job announcement and/or job description and matching these needs with your key skills and qualifications. Let the employer know what you can offer the company, not what you want from the company. In the paragraph where you are communicating your key skills and experience, refer the reader to the attached résumé. Do not duplicate what is already listed on your résumé; instead, emphasize your experience and key skills. Although it is acceptable to utilize the words "I and my" in a cover letter, be careful to not begin most of your sentences with the word "I". Instead, focus the attention toward the employer. This puts the company first and makes its needs more important. Attempt to begin a sentence with what the company will receive with your skills. For example:

Instead of writing, "*I* am proficient in Word,"

Write, "*Your* company will benefit from my proficiency in Word."

Address the cover letter to a specific person. This should be the person who will be making the hiring decision. Do not address your cover letter to a department, the company name, or "to whom it may concern." Call the company and ask for a specific name and title, identifying the appropriate spelling and gender. If you have conducted research and still cannot secure a specific name, use a subject line instead of a salutation. For example, instead of writing, "To Whom It May Concern," write, "Subject: Account Clerk Position." If you have talked to a specific person at your target company, refer to the previous communication. Include the specific position you are seeking in your cover letter and how you learned about the job opening. At the end of your cover letter, request an interview (not the job). Do not write that you look forward to the employer contacting you. Display initiative by stating that you will follow up on your request for an interview within the next week. Include an enclosure notation for your résumé and close courteously.

Cover Letter Setup, see Figure 8-8 on page 148

Use the proper business-letter format for your cover letter. Each word and paragraph in your cover letter must have a purpose. Your goal is to communicate how your knowledge, skills, abilities, and accomplishments fill a targeted company's needs and make the reader want to review your résumé. The cover-letter setup in Figure 8-8 and sample cover letters in Figures 8-9 and 8-10 will help you create a winning cover letter.

Cover Letter Example 1, see Figure 8-9 on page 149

Cover Letter Example 2, see Figure 8-10 on page 150

Print your cover letter on the same type of paper used for your résumé. Copy the information heading you created for your résumé and use it on your cover letter. This creates a consistent and professional visual appeal for your résumé package. Avoid making common mistakes, including typographical or grammatical errors, forgetting to include a date, or forgetting to sign the cover letter. Complete and grammatically correct sentences must be used on a cover letter. As with your résumé, have someone you trust proofread your letter before you send it to a potential employer. Any error communicates a lack of attention to detail. Even minor errors have the potential to disqualify you from securing an interview.

Tailoring Your Résumé and Cover Letter

Tailor your résumé and cover letter specifically to each job and company for which you are applying. Carefully review the target job announcement. If possible, secure a copy of the job description from the company's human resource department if it is not available or attached to the job posting. Identify key job skills that the position requires, and highlight the company needs with your skills. As you learned in step four of creating your résumé, utilize the O*Net website to identify key skills for your targeted position. If necessary, rearrange the order of the information presented on your résumé so that the key skills required for your target position are presented first. On your cover letter, emphasize your specific qualifications that match those required for the open position.

Although mentioned earlier, it cannot be stressed enough that a daytime phone number and e-mail address need to be listed on both the cover letter and résumé. Because most invitations for job interviews occur over the phone, your phone voice-mail and/or message machine need to be professional. Do not include musical introductions or any other greeting that would not make a positive first impression to a potential employer. Maintain a professional e-mail address to use in your job search.

Cory's friend Rebecca was a practical joker. Cory enjoyed calling Rebecca because her voice-mail message started with a joke or had some strange voice and/or music. However, the last time Cory called Rebecca, Cory noticed that Rebecca's message was normal. The next time Cory saw Rebecca, Cory asked Rebecca why her voice message was suddenly so serious. Rebecca explained that she had recently applied for a job and had been selected to interview. However, she was embarrassed because when the interviewer called to arrange the appointment, the interviewer left a message and also suggested that Rebecca change her voice-mail message to a more professional message.

Tips for Ex-Offenders

If you have served time in prison and are now attempting to reenter the workforce, you are to be congratulated for wanting to move forward with your life. Others have made poor choices in their past, and you have made restitution for yours. Be honest with the potential employer.

On your résumé, include all jobs you have held and skills you learned while incarcerated. List the correctional facility in place of the employer for these jobs. List all education, including degrees and courses you received while incarcerated. Include the educational institution that provided the training.

The employment application is a legal document. At the bottom of this document, applicants sign a statement that affirms that all information provided on the application is true. Therefore, you must not lie. If, after being hired, your employer discovers that you have lied on the application, you may be immediately terminated. The majority of applications ask if you have been convicted of a felony. Please note that arrests are not convictions. If you have been convicted of a felony, check "Yes." The application should also have a space to write a statement after the felony question. Do not leave this space blank. In this space, write, "Will explain in detail during interview."

Workplace Dos and Don'ts

Do keep your résumé updated with skills and accomplishments	*Don't* wait until the last minute to update your résumé
Do change your résumé format after you have gained work experience	*Don't* use outdated reference names and letters
Do use the correct format for your résumé	*Don't* send out a résumé or cover letter that has not been proofread by someone you can trust
Do check your résumé and cover letter for errors before sending them to employers	*Don't* forget to sign your cover letter

Susie Que
123 Someplace, Iowa City, IA 52240 • business-student@uiowa.edu • (123) 456-7891

EDUCATION
The University of Iowa, Iowa City, IA   May 2009
Bachelor of Business Administration: Management   Overall GPA: 3.3/4.0
Entrepreneurial Certificate
      Career Leadership Academy (four semester academic program)   December 2008
- Focused on developing leadership and employment skills
- Strengthened communication, teamwork, interpersonal, and presentation abilities

MANAGEMENT EXPERIENCE
Sales Management Intern   Summer 2008
INSYNC Business Solutions, Cedar Rapids, IA
- Interviewed and hired 5 sales associates
- Developed and implemented 3 week training program for all new part-time hires
- Assisted in accomplishing an overall department sales increase of 22%
- Worked with Sales Manager to identify target sales audience so to increase revenue

Customer Service Shift Manager   March 2006-May 2008
Hy-Vee Food Stores, Altoona, IA
- Oversaw weekend shift of part-time customer service representatives
- Coordinated bi-weekly schedule of 6 employees to maintain department coverage
- Oriented and trained 10 new employees over a 2 year period
- Assisted customers with check deposits, returns, and product location

ADDITIONAL EXPERIENCE
Office Assistant   June 2008-present
The University of Iowa Latino-Native American Cultural Center, Iowa City, IA
- Answered calls and assisted callers with center information
- Maintained organization budget for special events
- Assisted in the preparation of the monthly newsletter

Cashier   April 2001-August 2003
Hy-Vee Food Stores, Ankeny, IA
- Assisted over 100 customers daily with purchases of groceries, including check out and packaging
- Reconciled cash register with average daily cash flow of $4,000
- Assisted a group of 20 with yearly product inventory

LEADERSHIP & ACCOMPLISHMENTS
Vice President, Women in Business, The University of Iowa   2008-2009
The University of Iowa Deans List   2006-2008
Secretary, Leadership Council, Henry B. Tippie College of Business   2007-2008
Morale Captain, Dance Marathon, The University of Iowa   2005-2006

COMPUTER SKILLS
Word, Excel, Access, Publisher, Outlook, Adobe Illustrator

Courtesy of the Pomerantz Career Center.

Figure 8-1

Functional Résumé Layout

Ginger Snap

123 Someplace, Iowa City, IA 52240 ginger-snap@uiowa.edu   319-123-0000

Education
The University of Iowa, Iowa City, IA   Anticipated May 2015
Pre- Business

Work Experience
Cashier   June 2007 - August 2010
CiCi's Restaurant, Galena, IL
- Provided high quality customer service in a fast-paced environment
- Trained 4 new employees on customer service and daily tasks
- Supervised 3 wait staff to keep the restaurant running smoothly

Detasseler   Seasonally July 2004 - July 2006
Knightpickers Detasseling, Galena, IL
- Detasseled seed corn in the summer
- Achieved perfect attendance bonus

Leadership Experience
Career Leadership Academy, The University of Iowa   Spring 2012 - present
- Four semester academic program focused on developing leadership and employment skills
- Strengthened communication, teamwork, interpersonal, and presentation abilities
- Participated in career exploration, networking, and leadership development activities
- Attended employer panels and presentations by community leaders

Activities
Tippie Optimist Chapter, The University of Iowa   September 2010 – present
- Served as Pen Pal with 4th grade student
- Volunteered in after school program

High School Year Book, Galena High School   August 2008 – June 2010
- Raised $600 in advertisement sales from local businesses
- Designed 10 pages in yearbook

Community Service
Alternative Spring Break, New Orleans, LA   March 2010
- Participated in service trip to New Orleans
- Rebuilt houses with community members

Special Olympic Volunteer, Galena, IL   September 2007 – May 2009
- Helped athletes at 10 events
- Assisted at games, recorded scores, and handed out awards

Honors
National Honor Society   August 2008 – June 2010

Courtesy of the Pomerantz Career Center.

(continued)   Figure 8-1

Functional Résumé Layout

Jane Smith

123 Someplace, Iowa City, IA 52240
Phone: (123) 456-7891 Email: communication-student@uiowa.edu

OBJECTIVE

To obtain an internship for fall 2008 with Wells Fargo Event Planning utilizing my skills in graphic design and public relations to further the goals of the company

EDUCATION

The University of Iowa, Iowa City, IA   May 2013
B.A. Communication Studies, B.F.A Graphic Design
GPA 3.4/4.0
    Career Leadership Academy (four semester academic program)
        •Focused on developing leadership and employment skills
        •Strengthened communication, teamwork, interpersonal, and presentation abilities

SOFTWARE SKILLS

Adobe Photoshop	Macromedia Dreamweaver	Microsoft Publisher
Adobe Illustrator	Macromedia Flash	Microsoft FrontPage

INTERNSHIP EXPERIENCE

Public Relations Intern   May. 2012- Aug 2012
Ketchum, International   Chicago, IL
•Wrote and disseminated 5 newsletters, 3 media guides, and 10 news releases for clients
•Planned and facilitated 2 marketing events for new food and beverage client
•Developed a new public relations reporting device used to track and record client data daily

Marketing and Editing Intern   Aug. 2011- Dec. 2011
National Public Radio: WSUI-AM and KSUI-FM   Iowa City, IA
•Edited and created 30% of content for quarterly program guide with a circulation of 20,000
•Coordinated over 50 volunteers and tabulated donations during fundraisers
•Assisted with media relations and advertising campaigns for special events such as *Riverfest*

WORK EXPERIENCE

Hospitality Representative   Dec. 2009-May 2010
Walt Disney World Resorts   Lake Buena Vista, FL
•Greeted over 1,000 guests per day
•Acted as host for over 50 special events including *Disney's Magical Summer* program which served over 5,000 guests per month
•Provided over 100 customers with directions to attractions daily
•Completed Walt Disney Practicum Course in Public Relations

Cashier/ Lesson Instructor   May 2008 - May 2009
Cedar Rapids Recreation Department   Cedar Rapids, IA
•Cooperated with managers in training approximately 30 new cashiers, concession workers, and lesson instructors per summer season
•Helped reconcile cashier and concession area cash registers, often totaling in excess of $5,000 per day
•Taught swimming lessons to over 150 children
•Supervised cashier and concession workers' cleaning and closing procedures

ACTIVITIES

Volunteer, River Run	July 2008- Present
Member, 24/7 Campus Ministry	Jan. 2008- Present
Member, Public Relations Student Society of America (PRSSA)	Aug. 2010- Present
Secretary, Public Relations Student Society of America (PRSSA)	Jan. 2011- Present

Courtesy of the Pomerantz Career Center.

Figure 8-2

Functional Résumé Example with
Minimal Career Work Experience

Jane Doe Engineer

123 Any Street St. # · Any City, IA xxxxx · jane-doe@uiowa.edu · (xxx) xxx-xxxx

Education:

The University of Iowa, Iowa City, IA — May 2012
Major: Industrial Engineering — GPA: **3.00**/4.00
Minor: Business Management — Dean's List: Spring 2011

International Study: University of Indianapolis-Athens Campus, Athens, Greece — Summer 2010

Engineering Project Experiences:

Virtual International Project Team, John Deere Construction & Forestry, Dubuque, IA — Fall 2011
- Capstone senior design project on noise abatement of an Articulated Dump Truck
- Collaborated with a diverse group of engineers including international students in Marseille, France
- Designed and examined potential solutions using Pro-Engineer software

Teaching Assistant, Engineering Problem Solving I, Professor Peter O'Grady — Fall 2011
- Instructed classroom of 12 first year engineering students through assignments and projects
- Strategized in weekly update meetings over adjusting course guidelines as needed

Manufacturing Engineer Intern, The HON Company, Muscatine, IA — May 2011-August 2011
- Determined root cause analysis of shortage system, improved shortage ordering form and implemented delivery zones
- Defined refill tactics for shortage system, held trial in one department to verify the process was success in order to apply refill tactics plant wide
- Optimized board use in wood fabrication by determining rules and patterns saving ~$250,000 a year
- Analyzed and completed time studies in order to determine if cycle times of processes were accurate

Whirlpool Ergonomics Project, Human Factors — Fall 2010
- Examined and communicated with workers on pre-assembly line to determine preventable health hazards
- Tested different height adjustments on Digital Human Modeling software to minimize injury caused by bending/rotating during work process

Leadership Experiences:

President, Institute of Industrial Engineers Iowa Student Chapter — January 2011-Present
- Assembled proposal for a donation of funds to allow 24 chapter members to attend regional conference
- Expanded chapter involvement by coordinating seminars as well as professional and social meetings
- Delegated tasks to officers involving fundraising, maintaining websites, coordinating volunteers while planning 2013 IIE regional conference

Student Ambassador, The University of Iowa College of Engineering — July 2009- May 2011
- Educated prospective students and families about Iowa's abundant resources and opportunities
- Administered 6 Explore Engineering@Iowa programs for 200+ guests

Treasurer, Institute of Industrial Engineers Iowa Chapter — August 2009-January 2011
- Organized fundraising events to raise $900 for chapter activities
- Maintained groups bank accounts, filed taxes and completed necessary financial forms

Mentor, Women in Science &Engineering — July 2009-Present
- Inspired first year engineering students to access resources on campus and provided support
- Counseled mentees through enrichment workshops and time management strategies

Dance Marathon
Morale Captain Assistant, Family Representative & Development Committee — October 2008-February 2011

Career Leadership Academy — Fall 2009-Spring 2011
- Four semester academic program focused on developing leadership, teamwork and communication skills
- Participated in networking and leadership development activities
- Coordinated community service project to benefit the Domestic Violence Intervention Program

Professional Activities:

The Leadership Institute   Society of Women Engineers   Leadershape   Institute of Industrial Engineers

Courtesy of the Pomerantz Career Center.

Figure 8-3

Functional Résumé Example without Career Work Experience

Health Bio Student
123 Someplace Street, Iowa City, IA 52402
HealthandBio-student@uiowa.edu
(123) 123-4567

EDUCATION
Bachelor of Science in Health Promotion   May 2014
The University of Iowa, Iowa City, IA
GPA: 3.9/4.0

A.A. General Studies   May 2012
Kirkwood Community College, Cedar Rapids, IA

INSTRUMENTAL AND LABORATORY TECHNIQUES

GC-MS	GC-FID	HPLC
NMR	LSC	UV-VIS spectrometer
GE gamma ray defectors	PCR	IR spectrometer

RESEARCH EXPERIENCE
Research Assistant   August 2013 – Present
The University of Iowa Hospitals and Clinics, Iowa City, IA
- Perform experiment-related activities including maintenance of cultured cell lines, stable and transient DNA, cell fractionation and generation of antibodies
- Amplify RNA with the polymerase chain reaction and separated DNA with gel electrophoresis
- Compile over 50 lab reports every week for analysis
- Gather, analyze, and interpret data and assisted in developing presentations

Chemistry Intern   May 2012 – July 2012
XYZ Laboratories, Chicago, IL
- Organized layout of new chemical storage room and setup chemical database
- Performed identifications of samples by IR and physical testing of samples
- Assisted in Standard Operation Procedure composition and editing
- Prepared buffers, agars, and solutions for over 30 tests each week

LEADERSHIP EXPERIENCE
Participant   Fall 2011 – Spring 2012
Career Leadership Academy, The University of Iowa, Iowa City, IA

- Selected to partake in a two-year academic course focused on developing leadership and employment skills via activities focused on career exploration, networking, interviewing, resume building and leadership
- Developed communication, teamwork, interpersonal, and presentation abilities over the course of the program
- Coordinated a community service project with 10 CLA classmates for the Best Buddies organization pairing local children and college students together for a bowling tournament

WORK EXPERIENCE
Building Supervisor   Fall 2010 – Present
Recreation Services, Iowa City, IA
- Manage opening and closing procedures of Recreation Building to ensure accuracy and safety
- Communicate with over 50 customers daily about questions and complaints
- Handle cash and credit transactions, sell memberships, and reconcile cash register each shift
- Enforce rules and regulations by monitoring guest on the athletic fields and courts

Courtesy of the Pomerantz Career Center.

Figure 8-4

Chronological Résumé Layout

SALLY SMITH STUDENT

1234 Someplace Street ▪ Iowa City, IA 52242 ▪ sallysmith-student@uiowa.edu ▪ 123 . 123 . 1234

EDUCATION

University of Iowa, Iowa City, IA   May 2013
Bachelor of Science
Major: Nursing Minor: Psychology
GPA: 3.52 / 4.00

LICENSES AND CERTIFICATION:
- RN (anticipated 6/2013)
- BLS (CPR/AED)
- CNA

CLINICAL ROTATIONS:
- 225 Hour Senior Internship, Spring 2013, Cardiac/Surgical ICU (Mercy Medical Center, Des Moines)
- Medical/Surgical (Mercy, Iowa City)
- Pediatrics Cardiology (UIHC)
- Geriatrics (UIHC and Mercy, Iowa City)
- Respiratory Specialty Care Unit (UIHC)
- Home Care (Mercy, Cedar Rapids)
- Adult Neuropsychiatric Unit (UIHC)
- Public Health (UIHC, Cedar Rapids High Schools, Iowa City Elementary School)

NURSING/HEALTH CARE EXPERIENCE:

Mercy Medical Center, Des Moines, Iowa   January 2013-Present
Senior Internship, Cardiac/Surgical Intensive Care Unit
- Admit and provide nursing care to critically ill patients who have undergone complex cardiac surgeries
- Assess/monitor patients and assist with transfer to telemetry floor
- Collect vital signs and blood glucoses for 10 patients each shift

Mercy Hospital, Iowa City, IA   March 2011-January 2012
Monitor Technician, Telemetry Unit
- Completed classes and tests prior to working on cardiac rhythms and interpretation of EKGs
- Completed 40 hours of orientation with current monitor technician prior to working on my own
- Monitored patients on telemetry unit and medical/surgical unit
- Printed, read, and posted strips on each floor in patient's chart

LEADERSHIP EXPERIENCE

Career Leadership Academy, The University of Iowa, Iowa City, IA   Fall 2011 – Spring 2012
Participant
- Completed the four-semester academic program focused on developing leadership and professional growth
- Strengthened communication, teamwork, interpersonal, and presentational skills through activities such as a campus wide community service project, interactive teams courses, and service-based group speeches
- Participated in career exploration, networking, and leadership development activities

VOLUNTEER EXPERIENCE

Dance Marathon, Iowa City, IA   Spring 2012
Volunteer
- Raised $400 individually, contributing to a total amount of over $1 million for The Children's Miracle Network
- Interacted with cancer survivors and their families to learn about the cause and where the contributions go
- Volunteered in monthly activities aimed at increasing awareness of CMN and fundraising for the main event

Courtesy of the Pomerantz Career Center.

Figure 8-5

Chronological Résumé
Example with Degree

Art P. Student

123 Someplace Street
Iowa City, IA 52241
(123) 123-1234
performingarts-student@uiowa.edu

OBJECTIVE	To obtain an internship for the Summer of 2013 with Goodman Theatre utilizing my skills in performance and administration to further the goals of the Theatre

EDUCATION **The University of Iowa,** Iowa City, IA
B.A. Theatre Arts   Anticipated May 2014
Dean's List, 2 semesters
GPA: 3.4/4.0

Career Leadership Academy   Dec. 2013
• Four semester academic program
• Focus on developing leadership and employment skills
• Strengthen communication, teamwork, interpersonal, and presentation abilities

COURSE   Art of the Theatre   History of Theatre and Drama
HIGHLIGHTS   Acting I and II   Theatre Movement

RELATED   **Playwrights' Workshop Assistant,** Iowa City, IA
EXPERIENCE   The University of Iowa   Aug. 2012 to May 2012
• Coordinated all guest artist travel, scheduling, and orientation
• Organized and implemented the Playwrights' Workshop schedule
• Coordinated weekly play readings and discussions

Box Office Assistant, Hancher Auditorium
The University of Iowa, Iowa City, IA   Aug. 2011 to Dec. 2011
• Recruited and trained over 20 volunteer ushers
• Addressed ticketing problems and seat requests

OTHER
EXPERIENCE   **Clerk,** Iowa City, IA
Mercy Hospital, Department of Pediatrics   Aug. 2011 to Dec. 2011
• Updated hospital wide database with employee medical history
• Distributed paychecks to all divisions of pediatric staff on a bi-weekly basis
• Performed closing responsibilities for pediatric administrative offices

TEACHING &
AWARDS   Christian Youth Theatre-Chicago, Leader   Summers 2011-present
Tennessee Williams Scholarship Recipient   2012-present

Courtesy of the Pomerantz Career Center.

Figure 8-6

Chronological Résumé
Example with No Degree

Psy Chi Student

123 Someplace Street, Iowa City, IA 52242   123-123-1234   psychology-student@uiowa.edu

EDUCATION

The University of Iowa, Iowa City, IA   May 2011
Bachelor of Arts: Psychology   Minor: Spanish
GPA: 3.9/4.0

La Universidad de Guanajuato, Guanajuato, Mexico   Summer 2010
Spanish Language & Literature   Study Abroad

CLINICAL EXPERIENCE

Intern   Aug. 2009-May 2010
Adoption and Attachment Treatment Center of Iowa, Iowa City, IA
- Administered & scored psychological testing
- Co-facilitated group therapy focusing on social skills & emotional regulation
- Assisted with behavioral interventions with children; population served included children with attachment difficulties, trauma & loss histories, ADHD, Asperger & oppositional defiant tendencies
- Trained in safe physical restraint
- Assisted with assessment of individual & group skills
- Provided children with play-directed activities to help children process feelings

RESEARCH EXPERIENCE

Research Assistant   Jan. 2009-May 2009
Iowa Depression & Clinical Research Center, Iowa City, IA
- Screened women for postpartum depression through inventories including the PHQ-9 and PRAMS-6
- Recruited participants for studies through phone interviews
- Assisted in data analysis and entry
- Presented scholarly articles of recent research findings in clinical psychology
- Attended weekly lab meetings to discuss research findings and progress

LEADERSHIP EXPERIENCE

Student
Career Leadership Academy   Jan. 2008-Present
- Four-semester academic program focused on developing leadership and employment skills
- Strengthened communication, teamwork, interpersonal, and presentation abilities
- Participated in career exploration, networking, and leadership development activities
- Attended employer panels and presentations by community leaders

Student Health Representative   Aug. 2007-May 2008
The University of Iowa
- Conducted research that led to the development of the first on-campus pharmacy
- Attended meetings comprised of university professors, doctors, nurses, and graduate students
- Submitted formal statements about the need for all students to have access to affordable health care

LANGUAGE PROFICIENCES
Native in English, Near fluent in Spanish

Courtesy of the Pomerantz Career Center.

Figure 8-7

Psychology Résumé

Date of Letter

Employer's Name, Title
Company Name
Address
City, State Zip

Dear Mr./Ms./Dr.:

First Paragraph. Give the reason for the letter, the position for which you are applying, and how you learned of this position. Note any previous contact you may have had with the employer.

Second Paragraph. Tell why you are interested in the position, the organization, and its products or services. Indicate any research you have done on the position and/or the employer.

Third Paragraph. Refer to the attached resumé and highlight relevant aspects of your resumé. Emphasize the skills mentioned in the advertisement or on the job description. Provide specific reasons why the organization should hire you and what you can do to contribute to the organization's success.

Last Paragraph. Indicate your desire for an interview, and offer flexibility as to the time and place. Thank the employer for his or her consideration and express anticipation in meeting him or her. Include a phone number and e-mail address for contact.

Sincerely,

(Do not forget to sign your cover letter)

Your Name
Your Address
City, State Zip

Enclosure

Courtesy of the Pomerantz Career Center.

Figure 8-8

Cover Letter Setup

September 25, 2015

Owen Corporation
Attention Brandon Owen
435 East Chesny Street
Meadeville, PA 16335

Dear Mr. Owen:

As a recent accounting graduate of State University, Meadeville, I was delighted to learn from your web site of the available Junior Accountant position. The purpose of this letter is to express a strong interest in becoming an Owen Company Accountant at your Meadeville facility. In addition to possessing a B.S. degree in Business, Accounting, I am responsible and consider myself a leader.

Owen Company sponsors a variety of community services and employee recognition programs, which I have read a great deal about. Your company has earned my respect, as it has from much of the community for your involvement in the after-school programs in Meadeville Unified School District.

As you will see on the attached resumé, Owen Company would benefit from the skills I have learned throughout college. These include: general ledger and journal posting; Microsoft Word, Excel, and Access programs; Quickbooks; and accurate ten-key (150 cspm). In addition, I also offer a superior work ethic, strong communicative abilities, attention to detail, and a keen interest in upgrading my skills.

I am confident that my skills and abilities will make me an ideal candidate for a position in this field. I would appreciate an opportunity to meet with you to discuss how my skills can meet the needs of Owen Company. I will contact you by phone within the week to discuss the possibility of an interview.

Sincerely,

Suzie Kringle

Suzie Kringle
1234 Tolearn Avenue
Meadeville, PA 16335

Enclosure

Courtesy of the Pomerantz Career Center.

Figure 8-9

Cover Letter Example 1

HEIDI H. KRINGLE   1234 Tolearn Avenue, Meadeville, PA 16335
555-555-5555   hshore02@careersuccess.lns

September 21, 2015

Mr. Jared Bill
Austin Office Supplies
1122 Friendly Road
Meadeville, PA 93725

Dear Mr. Bill:

I recently spoke with Gene Armstrong, an employee at your company, and he recommended that I send you a copy of my resumé. Knowing the requirements for the position and that I am interested in working at this type of establishment, he felt that I would be an ideal candidate for your office assistant position.

My personal goal is to be a part of an organization such as yours that wants to excel in both growth and profit. I would welcome the opportunity to be employed at Austin's Office Supplies since this is the largest and best-known office supply company in the city. Your company has a reputation of excellent products and service.

Austin's Office Supplies would benefit from someone such as I who is accustomed to a fast-paced environment where deadlines are a priority and handling multiple jobs simultaneously is the norm. As you can see on the attached resumé, my previous jobs required me to be well organized, accurate, and friendly. I enjoy a challenge and work hard to attain my goals. Great customer skills are important in a business such as yours.

Nothing would please me more than to be a part of your team. I would like very much to discuss with you how I could contribute to your organization with my office skills and my dependability. I will contact you next week to arrange an interview. In the interim, I can be reached at 555-555-5555.

Sincerely,

Heidi H. Kringle

Heidi H. Kringle

Enclosure

Courtesy of the Pomerantz Career Center.

Figure 8-10

Cover Letter Example 2

Jolene M. Kringle

1234 Tolearn Avenue ■ Meadeville, PA 16335 ■ 555.555.5555
jmkringle@careersuccess.lns

Professional Reference List

Name	Relationship	Phone	E-mail	Mailing Address
Autumn Hart	Former Accounting Instructor, Hill Valley Technical College	555.555-1111	atmnhrt@hillvalley.scl	123 Hillvalley Clarkville, PA
Gloria Montes	Owner, El Montes Restaurant	555.555-1112	gloria@eatelmontes.fat	5432 Food Ct. Reedville, PA
Gary Solis	Floor Manager, Freshwide Marketing	555.555-1113	solisg@freshwide.fruit	2220 Tulare Lewis, PA
Patty Negoro	Office Manager, Starlight Produce	555.555-1114	pattyn@starlight.sun	444 Adoline Lewis, PA

Courtesy of the Pomerantz Career Center.

Figure 8-11

Tailored Package—
Reference List

Summary of Key Concepts

- A winning résumé makes it easy for potential employers to quickly and easily identify your skills and experience
- Update your résumé with new skills and accomplishments at least once a year
- Include both job-specific skills and transferable skills on your résumé
- Use the correct résumé layout for your career work experience
- A cover letter is most often an employer's first impression of you
- Check that your résumé and cover letter are free of typographical and grammatical errors
- Share your résumé electronically as a .pdf file to ensure the résumé layout is maintained

Key Terms

chronological résumé
functional résumé
  layout
résumé

cover letter
information heading
job-specific skills
soft skills

electronic formatted
  résumé
power words
transferable skills

If You Were the Boss

1. What would you look for first when reviewing a résumé?
2. What would your reaction be if you were reading a cover letter that had several typing and grammar errors?

Video Case Study: Résumé and Cover Letter Tips

This video presents expert advice on how to write a winning résumé and cover letter. To view these videos, visit the Student Resources: Professionalism section in www.mystudentsuccesslab.com. Then answer the following questions.

1. Share four common résumé mistakes and solutions.
2. Explain how to utilize a job announcement when preparing a résumé and cover letter.
3. Share four common cover-letter mistakes and solutions.
4. What information should be repeated in a cover letter that is already included on a résumé?

Web Links

www.onetcenter.org/
http://resume.monster.com
http://jobstar.org/tools/resume/index.htm
http://jobsearch.about.com/od/networking

Activities

Activity 8–1

Conduct an Internet search to identify five new power words to include in your résumé.

1. _____

2. _____

3. _____

4. _____

5. _____

Activity 8–2

Search for a job you would like to have when you graduate, and fill in the following information that will be used to tailor your résumé and create a cover letter.

Position for which you are applying	
How you learned about the job	
Any contact you have had with the employer or others about the job	
Why are you interested in this job?	
Why are you interested in this company?	
What products or services are provided?	
List relevant skills related to the job description	
List reasons this company should hire you	
Indicate your desire for an interview	
Indicate your flexibility for an interview (time and place)	

Activity 8–3

Using a word-processing program and the steps and/or exercises from this chapter, create a résumé for the job you found in Activity 8-2.

Activity 8–4

Using a word processing program and the information from this chapter, create a cover letter for the job you found in Activity 8-2.

Activity 8–5

Change the résumé from activity 8-3 to an electronic formatted résumé.

1. Update your résumé at least _____.

2. If you are starting a new career, create a résumé using the _____.

3. A/An _____ résumé format emphasizes your related work experience and skills.

4. _____ skills are those that are directly related to a specific job.

5. _____ skills are transferable from one job to the next.

6. Use _____ words whenever possible in your résumé; they describe your accomplishments in a lively and specific way.

7. The _____ is an introduction to your résumé.

Communication   Part I

by Lydia E. Anderson and Sandra B. Bolt

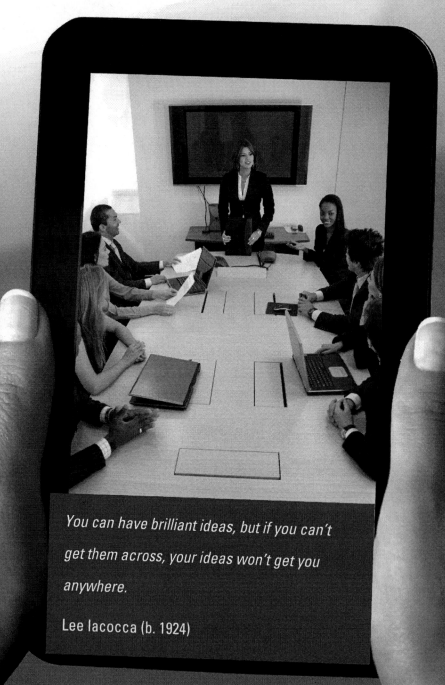

You can have brilliant ideas, but if you can't get them across, your ideas won't get you anywhere.

Lee Iacocca (b. 1924)

Objectives

- Define the impact effective *communication* has in the workplace
- Name the key elements of the communication process
- Name the three types of communication media
- Describe the dangers of becoming emotional at work
- Demonstrate proper formatting for *business letters* and *memos*
- Demonstrate basic telecommunication etiquette

If you answered "yes" to four or more of these questions, you are well on your way to mastering workplace communication. Communication success begins by presenting your message in a professional manner and focusing on the needs of the receiver.

Workplace Communication and Its Channels

Imagine going to work, sitting at your desk, and for one day sending and receiving no communication. If there were no face-to-face contact, no phones, no e-mails, no text messages, no meetings, and no memos to receive or write, business would come to a complete standstill. Even if you are talented at your job, if you cannot communicate with others, you will not succeed, much less keep a job. This chapter discusses the process and importance of effective communication in the workplace and provides information on how to improve workplace communication skills.

At work, you have an obligation to share appropriate, timely, and accurate information with your boss, your coworkers, and your customers. Improving communication skills is an ongoing process. Information is power. In regard to workplace communication, your goal is to be known as an overcommunicator.

While eating lunch with employees from other departments, Cory listened to others complain about how their bosses did such a poor job communicating with them. The employees complained that they never knew what was going on within the company. Cory had no reason to complain, because Cory has a manager who makes every effort to share whatever information he knows within the department. After each managers' meeting, Cory receives an e-mail outlining major topics that were discussed. During Cory's department meeting, Cory's manager reviews the information a second time and asks his employees if there are any additional questions. Cory appreciates the fact that the manager enjoys and values communicating important information with his employees.

In the workplace, there are two primary communication channels: formal and informal. Whether it is formal or informal communication, you have a professional obligation to share timely and relevant information with the appropriate people. **Formal communication** occurs through the formal (official) lines of authority. This includes communication within your immediate department, division, or throughout the company. Formal communication occurs either vertically or horizontally within an organization. Formal vertical communication flows down an organizational structure (via written correspondence, policies/procedures, and directives and announcements from management) or flows up an organizational structure (most commonly through reports, budgets, and requests). Formal horizontal communication occurs among individuals or departments at the same or close organizational levels.

The second type of communication channel is informal. **Informal communication** occurs among individuals without regard to the formal lines of authority. For example, while eating lunch with friends, you may learn of a new policy. A major element of the informal communication network is called the **grapevine.** The grapevine is an informal network where employees discuss workplace issues of importance. Although the grapevine is an informal source of communication, it usually is not 100 percent accurate. While it is important to know about current events at work, do not contribute negative or inaccurate information to the grapevine. Do not make assumptions if the information is incomplete. If you are aware of the facts, clarify the information. If someone shares information that is harmful to the company or is particularly disturbing to you, you have a responsibility to approach your boss and ask him or her to verify the rumor.

When the grapevine is targeting individuals and their personal lives, it is called **gossip.** Gossip is personal information about individuals that is hurtful and inappropriate. Any time you contribute to negative conversation, you lose credibility with others. Spreading gossip reflects immaturity and unprofessional behavior. Should someone begin sharing gossip with you, politely interrupt and clarify the misinformation when necessary. Tell the individual that you do not want to hear gossip and/or transition the conversation to a more positive subject. You have a right to defend your coworkers from slander (individuals bad-mouthing others), just as you would expect coworkers to defend you. After a while, your colleagues will learn that you do not tolerate gossip at work and they will reconsider approaching you with gossip.

Refrain from speaking poorly of your coworkers and boss. As a result of human nature, you may not enjoy working with all of your colleagues and bosses. You do not have to like everyone at work, but everyone needs to be treated with respect. Even if someone speaks poorly of you, do not reciprocate the bad behavior. It only displays immaturity on your part and communicates distrust to your colleagues.

The Communication Process

Communication is the process of a sender transmitting a message to a receiver with the purpose of creating mutual understanding. As simple as this definition is, a lot of barriers hinder the process of creating mutual understanding and successful communication. Communication is important for maintaining good human relations. Without basic communication skills, processes break down and an organization may collapse. This is why you need to know and understand the communication process (see Figure 9-1).

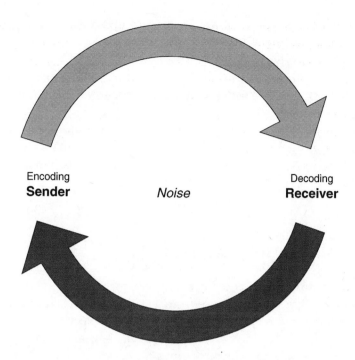

Figure 9-1

Communication Process

Encoding
Sender

Noise

Decoding
Receiver

Communication begins with a **sender** wanting to convey a message. The sender must identify what message needs to be sent and how best to transmit this message. The sender has several options for sending the message. The message can be sent verbally, in written form, or nonverbally. Identifying the message and how it will be sent is called **encoding.**

Once the sender encodes the message, the message is sent to a receiver. **Decoding** is when the receiver interprets the message. The receiver then sends **feedback** on the sender's message based upon the receiver's interpretation of the original message.

Several barriers may cause the communication process to break down. The first barrier to overcome is clearly identifying the message to be sent. Once the message is identified, the sender needs to determine how best to send (encode) the message in a manner that will be properly interpreted (decoded) by the receiver. If the sender is not a strong communicator, his or her verbal, written, or nonverbal communication may be misinterpreted by the receiver because the message was doomed before it was even sent. The receiver contributes to the communication breakdown if he or she incorrectly interprets the message.

Another barrier to effective communication is **noise.** Noise is anything that interrupts or interferes with the communication process. The noise can be audible (you can actually hear it with your ears), or the noise can occur through other means, such as visual, mental, touch, or smell. Noise may also include emotions such as hurt, anger, joy, sadness, or surprise.

A supervisor in another department really irritates Cory. Cory has never shared this annoyance with anyone. One day, Cory was asked to attend a meeting led by the irritating supervisor. As Cory sat in the meeting, Cory had a hard time focusing on the message. Cory's mind was wandering through mental noise. At the end of the meeting, Cory was embarrassed that there were no notes to share. Dislike for the irritating supervisor affected Cory's ability to listen and be a good receiver. Cory learned a hard lesson that day and made a commitment to be open to every communication, regardless of liking or disliking the sender.

Communication can be complete only if all of the components of the communication process work together to effectively send the message as they are intended to be sent. In order for this to occur, the sender must choose the right medium and overcome noise. The receiver must then be willing to accept the message and provide feedback to acknowledge that the message has been received correctly.

As previously stated, a key element of effective communication is the communication medium (how the message will be sent). Communication media include verbal, nonverbal, and written communication. Let us further explore these three types of communication media.

Verbal Communication and Listening

Verbal communication is the process of using words to send a message. The words you select are extremely important. If you use only basic words in your communications, you may appear uneducated or inexperienced. In contrast, if you use a highly developed vocabulary, you may appear intimidating or arrogant. If others do not know the definitions of the words you are using, they will most likely not ask for clarification for fear of appearing ignorant. Therefore, your intended message will fail. When selecting words for your message, identify whether these words are appropriate or if the words can be misinterpreted. Use proper English and grammar. Be as clear as possible in your intent and how you verbally convey your message. When people are nervous or excited, they frequently speak at a rapid pace. When you increase the speed of your speech, you increase the probability that your message will be misinterpreted. Your tone of voice also conveys or creates images. It adds to others' perception of you, which either enforces or detracts from your message.

Successful verbal communication involves listening. **Listening** is the act of hearing attentively. Learn to stop and listen. Too frequently, a person will have so much to say that he or she does not stop to provide the receiver time to respond. The receiver's response is the only way a sender can verify that a message has been properly received. Listening occurs not only with our ears, but also through our nonverbal responses. The three primary levels of listening are active listing, passive listening, and not listening at all. **Active listening** is when the receiver provides full attention to the sender without distraction. When the listener focuses his or her attention on the sender, an active listener will provide frequent positive feedback to the sender through nonverbal gestures such as nodding, eye contact, or other favorable body language. Favorable verbal feedback may also include rephrasing the message to ensure or clarify understanding. With **passive listening,** the receiver is selectively hearing parts of the message and is more focused on responding to what is being said instead of truly listening to the entire message being sent. Passive listening is sometimes called conversational listening. In today's society, we have so many inputs trying to attract our attention. As a result, we often get anxious to share our point of view in a conversation and fail to allow others in the conversation to complete their sentences by interrupting the sender. Interrupting is rude and disrespectful. Show others respect by not interrupting conversations. If you accidentally interrupt someone, immediately apologize and ask him or her to continue his or her statement. When a receiver fails to make any effort to hear or understand the sender's message, he or she is in the **nonlistening** mode and is allowing emotions, noise, or preconceptions to impede communication. Sometimes it is obvious the listener is not listening, because he or she either responds inappropriately or does not respond at all. While the ideal is to consistently be an active listener, we know this is not always possible. However, every effort should be made to strive toward active listening.

Silence is also an effective tool used in communication. Silence often makes individuals uncomfortable because our society is used to filling up silence with (sometimes useless) noise. Active listeners need time to digest what is being said and time to formulate a thoughtful response. Active listeners should wait at least three to five seconds before responding. At first, this may feel awkward, but you will quickly discover that you are becoming a better communicator because you are taking time to respond appropriately. Recognize that there are times when it is appropriate to not speak. Recognize and respect cultural differences in verbal communication in regard to word use and meaning.

Talk It Out

In what situations is it easy to be in "nonlistening" mode? What can an individual do to improve his or her listening skills in such a situation?

Nonverbal Communication

Nonverbal communication is what you communicate through body language. Even without uttering a word, you can still send a very strong message. Body language includes eye contact, facial expressions, tone of voice, and the positioning of your body. Nonverbal communication also includes the use of silence and space.

An obvious form of body language is eye contact. When you look someone in the eye, you are generally communicating honesty and sincerity. At other times, looking someone in the eye and coupling that look with a harsh tone of voice and an unfriendly facial expression may imply intimidation. In the United States, those who fail to look someone in the eye risk conveying to their receiver that they are not confident or, worse, are being dishonest. Make eye contact with your audience (individual or group), but do not stare. Staring is considered rude and intimidating. Actively work at making appropriate eye contact with your receiver. If your direct eye contact is making the receiver uncomfortable, he or she will look away. Be aware of his or her response and adapt your behavior appropriately.

Eye contact is part of the larger communication package of a facial expression. A receiver will find it difficult to interpret your eye contact as sincere and friendly when your message is accompanied by a frown. A smile has immense power and value. On the other hand, make sure you don't smile when listening to someone who is angry or upset. He or she may misinterpret your smile as condescending or as laughing at their distress. As explained previously, when actively listening, a nod implies that you are listening or agreeing with a sender's message. Even the positioning of your head can convey disagreement, confusion, or attentiveness.

Another element of nonverbal communication is the use and positioning of your body. Having your arms crossed in front of your body may be interpreted in several ways. You could be physically cold, angry, or uninterested. When you are not physically cold, having your arms crossed implies that you are creating a barrier between yourself and the other person. To eliminate any miscommunication, it is best to have your arms at your sides. Do not hide your hands in your pockets. In speaking with others, be aware of the positioning of your arms and those of your audience. Also, be aware of the positioning of your entire body. Turn your body toward those to whom you are speaking. It is considered rude to turn your back to or ignore someone when he or she is speaking. In this case, you are using your entire body to create a barrier. Avoid this type of rude behavior. This only communicates immaturity on your part.

Exercise 9-1   Body Language

With a partner, take turns communicating the following emotions through body language.

Emotion	Signal
1. Concern	
2. Distrust	
3. Eagerness	
4. Boredom	
5. Self-importance	

The use of your hands is extremely important in effective communication. Through varied positioning, you can use your hands to nonverbally ask someone to stop a behavior, be quiet, or reprimand him or her. Be aware of the positioning of your hands and fingers. In the United States, it is considered rude to point at someone with one finger. Many finger and hand gestures commonly used in the United States are quite offensive in other countries. If you have nervous gestures such as popping your knuckles, biting your nails, or continually tapping your fingers, take steps to eliminate these habits.

Apart from a professional handshake, touching another person at work is not acceptable. People in our society frequently place a hand on another's shoulder as a show of support. However, others could interpret that hand on the shoulder as a threat or sexual advance. Therefore, keep your hands to yourself.

Proxemics is the study of distance (space) between individuals and is also an important factor in body language. An individual's personal space is about one and one-half feet around him or her. The appropriate social space is four feet from an individual. Standing too close may be interpreted as intimidation or may imply intimacy. Neither is appropriate for the workplace. However, distancing yourself too far from someone may imply your unwillingness to communicate. Be aware of the space you allow between you and your receiver.

Another element that affects nonverbal communication is emotion. Make every attempt to not become emotional at work. However, reality may cause you to express emotions that oftentimes cannot be controlled. Try to control your emotions in public. If you feel you are beginning to cry or have an outburst of anger, excuse yourself. Find a private area and deal with your emotion. If you are crying or distraught, splash water on your face and regain control of your emotions. If you are getting angry, assess why you are angry, control your anger, and then create a strategy to regain control of how best to handle the situation in a professional manner. Any overt display of anger in the workplace is inappropriate, can damage workplace relationships, and could potentially jeopardize your job. When you become emotional at work, you lose your ability to logically deal with situations and risk losing your credibility and the trust of others. Practice effective stress management and think before you respond. Finally, recall our earlier discussion on the appropriate use of silence. Silence is perhaps one of the most important communication tools you have. Silence communicates to your audience that you are listening and are allowing the other party consideration. Not immediately responding to a message provides the sender time to clarify or rephrase a message.

There are many variables involved in effective nonverbal communication. Interpret body language within its entire context. For example, if you are communicating with a colleague with whom you have a positive working relationship and your coworker crosses his or her arms, your coworker is most likely cold. Consider the entire package: environment, relationship, and situation.

Concept Review and Application

Summary of Key Concepts

- Effective communication is necessary for workplace success
- The goal of communication is to create a mutual understanding between the sender and the receiver
- There are appropriate times to utilize both the formal and informal communication channels
- The communication process involves a sender, a receiver, noise, and feedback
- Listening and silence are effective tools for effective communication
- Thoughtfully consider the right words to increase the chance of successful written and verbal communication
- Because the receiver of your message will not have verbal and nonverbal assistance in interpreting your message, take great care with all written messages

Key Terms

active listening	communication	decoding
encoding	feedback	formal communication
gossip	grapevine	informal communication
listening	noise	nonlistening
nonverbal communication	passive listening	proxemics
sender	verbal communication	

If You Were the Boss

1. One of your employees uses bad grammar that is reflecting poorly on your department. How can you correct the situation?
2. Employees keep saying they do not know what is going on at work. What steps would you take to increase workplace communication?

Video Case Study: Language in the Office

This video addresses language in the office. To view these videos, visit the Student Resources: Professionalism section in www.mystudentsuccesslab.com. Then answer the following questions:

1. In the opening dialog between John and Regina, what specific advice would you give John? Why? What advice would you give Regina? Why?
2. Did Regina appropriately handle her telephone call? Please explain your answer.
3. Is the dialog between John and Brian appropriate? Provide specific examples.
4. Name two examples of how Brian could improve his language when speaking with Gerald.

Web Links

http://owl.english.purdue.edu/handouts/pw/p_memo.html
http://blog.justjobs.com/using-foul-language-in-the-workplace-can-get-you-fired/

Activities

Activity 9-1

Without infringing on someone's privacy, discreetly observe a stranger's body language for approximately five minutes. Stay far enough away to not hear him or her speak. Name at least two assumptions you can make by simply watching the person's gestures, movements, and expressions.

Gesture, Movement, or Expression	Assumption
1.	
2.	
3.	

Activity 9-2

Watch a television news show for a half hour. Document at least two facial expressions of an individual being interviewed. Did the individual's facial expressions match his or her statements?

Facial Expression	Match Statements: Yes or No
1.	
2.	

Sample Exam Questions

1. The two types of workplace communication include _____ and _____ communication.

2. A major form of the informal communication network is called _____.

3. When the _____ is targeting individuals and their personal lives, it is called _____.

4. When _____ are displayed at work, it becomes difficult to think and behave in a logical manner.

5. Nonverbal communication is what we communicate through our _____.

6. _____ communicates to your audience that you are listening and are allowing the other party consideration.

7. Check that all _____ is error-free by proofreading prior to sending.

What's My Communication Style?

chapter **10**

by E.M. Russo

Courtesy of Shutterstock.

Communication

Communication is but one manifestation of personality style, but it warrants its own consideration because of its importance in our day-to-day interactions. If we can get a grasp on how we communicate and how others communicate, we can adapt and improve the reception of the messages we are trying to get across.

What is communication? Most people think of two or more people engaged in conversation. But communication is at once more complex and more simple than conversation. At the simplest level, communication occurs when a message is sent by a sender and received by a receiver. As simple as this may sound, the complication occurs because the message sent does not always equal the message received. The sender may be too subtle or the receiver may not pay attention. There are many ways in which the message can get changed on its way to the receiver. For example, I may intend to communicate that I am supportive by saying, "I am sorry that happened to you," but you may receive the message that I am being insincere. This misinterpretation occurs because the person receiving a message is not a blank slate. A receiver has his or her own history and style and interprets any messages coming his or her way. Communication is actually a shared social experience between two or more people who each have their own expectations and intentions (Coyle, 1993).

To make matters even more complicated, as the receiver interprets the message, the sender reads the receiver's reaction and may adjust the message. Facilitators do this all the time. As they read facial expressions and body language, they may realize that the audience is bored or is not following what they are saying. They then adjust what they say and how they say it to increase audience attentiveness. The constant give and take between sender and receiver makes communication dynamic and living.

Another reason communication is complicated is because it can take many forms other than the spoken word. And even the spoken word, our verbal communication, is not always clear-cut. In *What's My Communication Style?* we focus on four different forms of communication: verbal, paraverbal, body language, and personal space.

Verbal

Although we choose the words we use in a message, and therefore have a great degree of control over those words, the meaning of the words may not be shared by those with whom we are speaking. We tend to believe that everyone shares the same interpretation of words, but this is not always true. Because of differences in age, experience, and background, words have different meanings to different people. The words we use and the way in which we use them is determined to a great degree by our communication style.

Paraverbal

It is not just the words we say but the way we say them that communicates meaning. The way in which something is said is called paraverbal communication. It includes how quickly one speaks, pauses, tone of voice, and intensity of voice. For example, fast-paced speech often indicates excitement or anxiety. You may say the words, "I'm calm. I'm calm. I'm calm." But if you say this very quickly in a high-pitched tone, people will not perceive you as calm.

As receivers of messages, we use paraverbal cues to help us interpret the meaning of what someone is saying. In fact, without paraverbal cues, we would be unable to interpret speech forms such as sarcasm. Sarcasm occurs when someone says one thing (e.g., "That's nice"), but means something entirely different, like "I'm bored," or, "That is not nice at all." Interestingly, taking turns in conversation is also determined by paraverbal cues. When someone trails off or lowers his or her voice, that can be a sign that it is the other party's turn to speak.

Like verbal communication, paraverbal communication is determined in many ways by our communication style. As we will see, a mismatch of styles can make interpretation more difficult.

Body Language

We do not have to use words at all to communicate. The way we stand, the way we shake hands, and the way we maintain eye contact are all forms of body language and all communicate meaning to others. Body language can indicate attentiveness, emotions, and reactions. Eye contact is one of the most telling of the body language cues. It can either support or contradict verbal communication. For example, you may say you are interested but look around the room as another is speaking. Your verbal and your body language cues are contradicting each other. Facial expressions are another telling sign. Immediate facial expression reactions often communicate more than words could, as in, "It's written all over your face." Body movements, gestures, and touch are other forms of body language that can enhance verbal communication, contradict it, or stand alone as a piece of communication.

Body language is also heavily influenced by style. Our preferences for eye contact, gesturing, and touch are usually quite pronounced. It becomes easier to read another person's body language message if you know his or her style.

Personal Space

The final type of communication is the use of personal space. This includes not only the space between you and others, but also how you arrange your work space, your personal appearance, and your choice of decorations. Interpersonal distance, or how close people are physically to one another, has been studied extensively. There are four zones of interpersonal distance: intimate, personal, social, and public. How close we prefer to be to others is a function of our styles.

Whether your work or home space is cluttered or neat, organized or disorganized, communicates to others what your priorities are and what type of person you are. Again, this is usually a function of your communication style.

All four forms of communication are important in our ability to send messages. Verbal communication is the most easily and the most often controlled, but it is beneficial to think about how you use the other forms of communication and how others are interpreting your messages. How style influences each form of communication is covered in Figure 10-4.

Why Be Concerned about Style?

Personality style is important in several aspects of organizational and personal life. Style affects our interaction with others (Hunsaker & Alessandra, 1980). People with different styles have different priorities and work or function at different paces. These differences can create problems if they remain under the surface. If Joe likes to be slow and thorough and Jane likes to be fast and decisive, their working relationship will be stressful unless they are aware of each other's preferences. Knowledge of styles prevents misinterpretations and frustrations.

Knowledge of style helps people to interpret others' actions (Snavely, 1981). If people are aware of another person's typical behaviors, they will take these behaviors into account when interpreting the other person's actions. For example, if Fred is generally a friendly and outgoing person, the fact that he gives you an enthusiastic hello should not be interpreted as a sign of deep friendship. Fred probably gives an enthusiastic hello to most co-workers. If, on the other hand, Fred is a private person and gives you an enthusiastic hello, that might be taken correctly as a sign of friendship. Knowledge of style sets up expectations of certain behaviors. When the unexpected occurs, people can more accurately attach meaning to it.

How people handle their styles determines their success. People who prefer logical, straightforward assignments should try to work in such an environment. Those who thrive on working with people might want to work in a field in which they deal with the public. Being aware of one's own style allows a person to choose the right situation for him or her and to be aware of how best to use his or her behavioral tendencies in any situation.

Dimensions of Style

The concept of style and the basic dimensions of style date back to Jung's 1914 work (Jung, 1971). Since his time, many researchers have examined personality styles (e.g., Marston, 1979; Merril & Reid, 1981; and Schutz, 1966). One clear finding from this research is that the number of styles is not unlimited. Although each individual is unique, there are definite commonalities. In fact, most research has found two basic dimensions of style, which we have chosen to refer to as *assertiveness* and *expressiveness*.

Assertiveness is the effort that a person makes to influence or control the thoughts or actions of others. People who are assertive tell others how things should be. They are task-oriented, active, confident, and ambitious. People who are not assertive ask others how things should be. They are reserved, easygoing, private, and deliberate.

Expressiveness is the effort that a person makes to control his or her emotions and feelings when relating to others. People who are expressive display their emotions. They are versatile, sociable, and extroverted. People who are not expressive control their emotions. They are dogmatic, controlled, and quiet.

One's personality style is determined by his or her assertiveness and expressiveness. Four styles result from combining assertiveness and expressiveness. Different names have been given to these styles (see Alessandra & Hunsaker, 1993; and Wheeless & Lashbrook, 1987 as examples). We have chosen to label them *Direct, Spirited, Considerate,* and *Systematic.* They are shown in the model on the next page. This model forms the basis of *What's My Communication Style?*

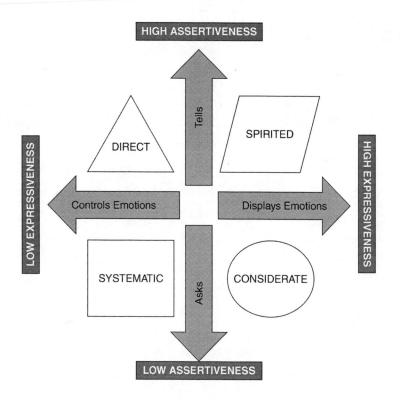

Figure 10-1

The Four Communication
Styles

Style Strengths

Each style has definite strengths that are evident in communication. Knowledge of these strengths allows people to draw on them and to find situations in which the strengths are a benefit. Figure 10-2 contains a quick list of the strengths of each style. More detailed descriptions follow.

Direct   People with a Direct style tend to take charge of their lives. They prefer to be in control and are quite capable of working independently. They are decisive in their actions and are high achievers. Direct people thrive on competition. They enjoy the challenge of a fight and enjoy the win even more. They maintain a fast pace as they work single-mindedly on their goals. Direct people are good in positions of authority in which independence is required. They possess strong leadership skills and have an ability to get things done. They are not afraid to take risks to get what they want.

Spirited   People with a Spirited style are enthusiastic and friendly. They prefer to be around other people and thrive in the spotlight. Because of their positive focus and their lively nature, they are able to generate motivation and excitement in others. Spirited people work at a fast pace because they prefer stimulation. They are well suited to high-profile positions in which public presentations are important. The spontaneity of Spirited people promotes quick and decisive action. They are good at building alliances and using relationships to accomplish work.

Considerate   People with a Considerate style value warm, personal relationships. They often have good counseling skills and others come

Direct

△ Gets to the bottom line
△ Speaks forcefully
△ Maintains eye contact
△ Presents position strongly

Spirited

☐ Is persuasive
☐ Is a good storyteller
☐ Focuses on the big picture
☐ Uses motivational speech

Considerate

○ Listens well
○ Is a good counselor
○ Uses supportive language
○ Builds trust

Systematic

☐ Presents precisely
☐ Focuses on facts
☐ Is efficient in speech
☐ Has a well-organized work space

Figure 10-2

Style Strengths

to them for support because they are good listeners. Considerate people are cooperative and enjoy being part of a team. They are reliable and steady. Because they are considerate, they are always aware of others' feelings. Considerate people work best in an environment in which teamwork is essential. Their ability to help others makes them suitable for any of the helping professions in which they can care for others.

Systematic   People with a Systematic style place a heavy emphasis on accuracy and objectivity. They make their decisions based on facts and attempt to leave emotions out of them. Their reliance on data makes them excellent problem solvers. They tend to be persistent in their analyses, maintaining a critical focus throughout their work. Systematic people are orderly and prefer to work in an organized environment with clear guidelines. Because Systematic people can work independently and follow-through on tasks, they are well-suited for independent, technical jobs.

Style Trouble Spots

All of the four styles contain potential trouble spots. Some of these trouble spots stem from the simple fact that any good thing taken to an extreme can become a problem. For example, no one would question that being friendly is a positive attribute. If someone is overly friendly to the point of losing professional decorum, however, that attribute can become a negative. People who are under stress tend to take their style behaviors to an extreme. In addition, a strong emphasis on one style generally means a weakness in another. For example, a highly objective person may find him- or herself neglecting people's feelings. Some of the potential trouble spots for each style are shown in Figure 10-3, with descriptions following.

Direct   Direct people when stressed may cross the line from controlling to overbearing. Their need to get things done quickly may cause

Direct

Δ Is a poor listener
Δ Is impatient with others
Δ Does not heed advice
Δ Likes to argue

Spirited

❑ Does not hear details
❑ Tends to exaggerate
❑ Generalizes
❑ Can be overdramatic

Considerate

○ Avoids conflict
○ Gives in easily
○ Keeps opinions to oneself
○ Overemphasizes feelings

Systematic

❑ Focuses too much on details
❑ Fears personal disclosure
❑ Can be terse
❑ Uses little variety in vocal tones

Figure 10-3

Style Trouble Spots

them to overlook fine details, which may lead to mistakes. Focusing on feelings is not a strength of Direct people and personal feelings may be pushed aside. People with a Direct style may have a tendency to view every situation as competitive. This view may make others uncomfortable and create needless tension. Direct people also may become workaholics if left unchecked.

Spirited Spirited people when stressed tend to intensify their verbal behavior. They may exaggerate for effect in their stories. They also might respond to criticism with verbal attacks. They often generalize and gloss over important details because of their enthusiastic support of an idea. Spirited people are rarely concerned with time constraints and may not control the use of their time.

Considerate Considerate people when stressed may try to assure themselves by sticking with what is comfortable and avoiding change. Because Considerate people dislike conflict they may tell others what others wish to hear. This avoidance of conflict may result in Considerate people not achieving what they want. Unfortunately their unachieved wants and needs may linger under the surface and they may become resentful. Future interaction with those who thwarted the Considerate person will be tense.

Systematic Systematic people when stressed may continually seek more information to make them feel confident. This information seeking may hide their avoidance of an issue or their withdrawal from others. It may also delay decision making. Because Systematic people are uncomfortable with emotions, they may avoid having to express them at all costs. They tend to put quality and accuracy ahead of feelings, even if it might hurt others. Systematic people often appear impersonal to others.

The following chart shows how each communication style influences the different forms of communication.

	Direct	Spirited	Considerate	Systematic
Verbal	❑ decisive ❑ direct speech ❑ doesn't stop to say hello	❑ expresses opinions readily ❑ generalizes ❑ persuasive	❑ listens ❑ close, personal language ❑ supportive language	❑ focuses on specific details ❑ precise language ❑ avoids emotions
Paraverbal	❑ speaks quickly ❑ loud tones ❑ formal speech	❑ lots of voice inflection ❑ animated ❑ loud tones	❑ speaks slowly ❑ soft tones ❑ patient speech	❑ little vocal variety ❑ brief speech ❑ even delivery
Body Language	❑ direct eye contact ❑ firm handshake ❑ bold visual appearance	❑ quick actions ❑ lots of body movement ❑ enthusiastic handshake	❑ gentle handshake ❑ likes hugging ❑ slow movement	❑ poker face ❑ controlled movement ❑ avoids touching
Personal Space	❑ keeps physical distance ❑ displays planning calendars in work space ❑ work space suggests power	❑ cluttered workspace ❑ personal slogans in office ❑ likes close physical space	❑ family pictures in workspace ❑ likes side-by-side seating ❑ carries sentimental items	❑ a strong sense of personal space ❑ charts, graphs in office ❑ tidy desktop

Figure 10-4

Influence of Communication Style on Communication

Interacting with Different Styles

People with different styles often develop misunderstandings that result more from their style differences than from real differences in their beliefs or opinions. For example, a fast-paced Spirited person and a slow-paced Systematic person may have tense interactions because of the different speeds at which they make decisions.

Although each of us has a predominant style, a certain amount of flexibility is necessary to communicate with people who have different styles. This means understanding others' styles and being willing and able to adjust one's style to interact more effectively with them.

Understanding others' styles involves observing their behavior. Hunsaker & Alessandra (1980) describe a useful observation process. First, observe the person's behavior and note the degree of assertiveness and expressiveness used.

Assertive people maintain steady eye contact, make emphatic statements, speak loudly and quickly, and are fast moving. People who are low in assertiveness do not communicate readily, use a low voice, speak slowly, and communicate hesitantly.

Expressive people show animated facial expressions, tell stories, share personal feelings, and seek contact. People who are low in expressiveness control their body movement, are disciplined with time, push for facts and details, and avoid contact.

Knowing how assertive and expressive a person is helps one to identify that person's style. The table below presents the styles in terms of assertiveness and expressiveness.

Direct = *High assertiveness, low expressiveness*
Spirited = *High assertiveness, high expressiveness*
Considerate = *Low assertiveness, high expressiveness*
Systematic = *Low assertiveness, low expressiveness*

Recognizing another's style allows us to make adjustments in our own behavior to accommodate that person's style. This in turn makes that person feel more at ease and helps us to achieve our goals more readily. For example, it will be much easier to convince a Systematic person to accept a decision if one is armed with concrete facts rather than general impressions. Even if one is a Spirited person who prefers general impressions, it will serve him or her well to be flexible in this situation. Behaviors that make interaction with each style type more effective are shown in Figure 10-5.

It takes some willingness and effort to expand beyond one's own style to interact with others. It is generally appreciated, however, and may make the difference between success and failure in an interaction.

Direct

Δ Focus on their goals and objectives
Δ Keep your relationship businesslike
Δ Argue facts, not personal feelings
Δ Be well-organized in your presentations
Δ Ask questions directly
Δ Speak at a relatively fast pace

Spirited

❑ Focus on opinions and inspiring ideas
❑ Be supportive of their ideas
❑ Don't hurry the discussion
❑ Engage in brainstorming
❑ Be entertaining and fast-moving
❑ Allow them to share their ideas freely

Considerate

○ Focus on your relationship
○ Be supportive of their feelings
○ Make sure you understand their needs
○ Be informal
○ Maintain a relaxed pace
○ Give them time to build trust in you

Systematic

❑ Focus on facts, not opinions
❑ Be thorough and organized
❑ Provide written evidence when possible
❑ Be systematic in your presentations
❑ Avoid gimmicks
❑ Allow time for analysis

Figure 10-5

Interacting with Different Styles

Ten Ways That "Good" Communication Styles Vary across Cultures

Task Orientation

It's important to take care of business without wasting excessive time on small talk and getting to know each other.

Clarity

It is best to be clear and specific in expressing and requesting information. Beating around the bush is annoying or a sign that people are evading the truth.

Face-to-Face Communication

Two people should work out their problems directly with each other.

Emphasis on Words

If something is important or on your mind, you should speak up.

Importance of Indvidual Opinion

People should express their individual points of view and opinions even if they differ from the beliefs or opinions held by others in the group.

Supportive Discusson

When disagreeing with or criticizing others, it's important to do so in a positive, supportive manner. A person may feel personally attached when someone else argues with her.

Expression of Emotion

It is okay to share feelings such as happiness, excitement, enthusiasm or sadness through words or facial expressions.

Detached/Objective Style

In meetings, people should stay rational and in control of their emotions. Becoming overly emotional takes away from the speaker's credibility and effectiveness.

Simplicity

It's best to simplify ideas, clarify thoughts, and avoid ambiguity.

Concrete

The best way to learn or to solve a problem is to examine and discuss concrete examples.

Relationship Orientation

Building relationships is more important than completing tasks. People cannot do business together until they have taken time to establish a relationship.

Indirect Speech

It is best to be vague and ambiguous when expressing information. Speaking in a direct, straightforward way is unnecessarily harsh and impolite.

Use of Third Party

The best way to work out problems between two people is to use an intermediary or go-between.

Empahsis on Context

If something is important, it should be left unsaid. Putting everything into words weakens communication and relationships.

Importance of Harmony

Disagreeing with others, pointing out mistakes, or insisting on personal opinions can undermine a group. It causes group disharmony and loss of face.

Critical Disussion

Arguing, debating, and criticizing ideas are enjoyable and acceptable conversational styles. One should point out the weakness in the other person's argument at this promotes the exchange of idea.

Suppression of Emotion

It is important and thoughtful to hide all personal feelings and opinions so that they are not evident in words or facial expressions.

Animated Style

Becoming louder or animated is a sign of involvement in the discussion. A person who remains unanimated during the discussion may be insincere or not interested in the topic.

Complexity

Simplicity should be distrusted. Complex communication reflects the depth of the topic.

Theoretical

The best way to learn or to solve a problem is to discuss the underlying theory and philosophy.

*Adapted from: Aguillar, L. & Stokes, L. (1996) *Multicultural customer service: Providing outstanding service across cultures.* Chicago: Times Mirror Higher Education Group, Inc.

Problem Solving

by Ciara Woods

Courtesy of Shutterstock.

chapter 11

Objectives

- The process

- Lessons learned through experience

- Tried and trusted techniques

You might feel that a lack of knowledge and experience is a stumbling block in solving a problem, but it can often be a huge advantage. When solving problems, imagination is just as important as information, so make use of your fresh approach and your lack of assumptions about the way things should be done. Often, challenging an assumption can turn obstacles into opportunities. Seeing things differently is a key skill and this chapter will give you the structure to feel confident enough to unleash your creativity. It will also outline some things you should bear in mind when solving a problem, as well as suggesting some useful problem-solving techniques.

The Process

Before you start to solve a 'problem', ask yourself two things: first, is there really a problem? And second, should you be trying to solve it?

- If there is no real problem why waste time trying to solve it? This may sound obvious, but it is amazing how many people do waste time.
- If there is a problem, you may not be expected to solve it or you may not have the time to. Maybe it's not you who should be solving this particular problem.

If you decide you should and can solve the question at hand, the following process should help:

1. **Identify the problem.**
   - Write down a description of the problem, answering all the who, why, what, where, when and how questions. Although this description may evolve over time, if you can state your problem in a clear and concise way, then you are halfway to solving it.
   - Don't get bogged down in understanding the cause of the problem at this early stage, as it is often very hard to discern.
   - Show your description of the problem to someone who is affected by it. Check with them that you have correctly understood it.
2. **Write down all the possible solutions.**
   - Think of as many ways of solving the problem as you can.
   - Ask other people what they think. Brainstorming is a fantastic way to generate lots of ideas in a short space of time. (See Techniques section.)
   - Try to be as specific and realistic as possible about proposed approaches.
3. **Evaluate each of these options.**
   - Look at each option from different perspectives. De Bono's Hats is a great way to do this. (See Techniques section.)
   - List the pros and cons for each option.
   - Eliminate options that don't make the grade or are unrealistic and highlight ones that look promising.
   - Consider your gut reaction (what solution feels intuitively right?) but don't make rash or emotional decisions and watch out for biases.

> **CHECK LIST**
>
> When evaluating the pros and cons, think through:
> ✓ What is likely to happen if you were to choose each option?
> ✓ What would the worst and best outcomes of making that choice be?
> ✓ How would people react to each option if it were chosen?
> ✓ Which option would resolve the problem long term?
> ✓ Which option is the most realistically attainable, given time, resources and costs?

4. **Select your best option.**
   - Ask the opinion of some relevant people as to which option they would choose.
   - Don't let deliberation become procrastination—make a choice.
   - Once you have decided on an option, let go of the others and move on.
5. **Make sure the solution can and will happen.**
   - Make the solution attainable. The solution must be real—a theoretical solution is no use. The infrastructure must exist for the solution (you need to work around what you are given).
   - Share the choice with people who will be affected and get their support. People who believe in what they are doing work much harder to make things succeed than people who don't.
6. **Plan the way forward.**
   - Think through and draw up a plan of what will need to be done, by whom and by when.
   - Make sure that the tasks are measurable (mark key milestones) and that the process can be easily checked.
   - Identify possible problems and have a contingency plan that you can put in place if things go wrong.
7. **Get feedback on the plan.**
   - Share the plan with the people who need to implement it and get their support. Adapt the solution if necessary.
8. **Monitor progress.**
   - Check how the plan is going on a regular basis.
   - Make the necessary changes if things are not going according to schedule.

> **Top Tip**
>
> KISS (Keep It Simple Stupid!) Try to make the solution as simple as possible. The more complex a solution gets, the harder it is to explain and the easier it is to get wrong.

> **Top Tip**
>
> Try to understand why things are not working out, don't just keep shifting the deadline. This is valuable information that you can use the next time you have to tackle a problem.

Lessons Learned through Experience

1. **Understand the problem.**
   - Admit it if you don't understand what exactly you are being asked to solve. Ask questions to clarify the situation and don't accept anything other than clear and distinct ideas.

- Keep asking questions until you have a clear understanding of what you are meant to do. It is better to understand the problem fully before you start to solve it, rather than pretend you understand and have to come crawling back later when you can't solve the problem.

2. **Manage the deadline.**
   - Break the problem into parts, prioritize them and deliver what you can first. If you try to deliver the whole thing in one go, you may end up delivering nothing for ages and your boss will not be impressed. Deliver, deliver, deliver is the quickest way to getting a job done.

CHECK LIST

When the problem lands on your desk, ask:

✓ What do I need to know to solve this?

✓ Whom can I talk to?

✓ What other resources are available to me?

✓ When does it need to be done?

✓ Who needs to be told the answer when it is solved?

Top Tip

Manage your boss's expectations by alerting him/her immediately if you are having problems meeting the deadline.

Top Tip

If at first you don't succeed, take a break!

3. **Get in the right state of mind.**
   - Find a quiet corner or an empty office and block everything else out. You need a clear head to think properly.

4. **Have patience with the problem.**
   - Don't give up if you can't solve the problem in the first 5 minutes.
   - Take a break (e.g. go for a walk or grab a coffee) if you are hitting a brick wall. A change of scenery is usually all that is needed to get the creative juices flowing again.

5. **Don't be overwhelmed.**
   - Never forget that you can always do something.

CHECK LIST

Start somewhere:

✓ Put all the concrete information you have down on paper.

✓ Draw a diagram/picture of the problem. Visualization often makes problems easier to understand.

✓ Break up the problem into smaller parts.

✓ Use some problem-solving techniques (see next section).

6. **Don't reinvent the wheel.**
   - Learn from the experiences of previous problems, be they ones you have solved personally or ones solved by someone else. It is usually quicker to find an answer that already exists than to create a new one.

7. **A problem shared is a problem solved.**
   - Never forget that you can easily be biased or blinkered, so ask as many people as you can (within reason) for their ideas. The more options you have, the better choice you can make.

- Some of the most valuable conversations result from random encounters (e.g. in corridors, on the way to lunch). You can gain a lot just by wandering around and talking to people. Always keep in touch with what everyone is doing.

8. **Be flexible.**
    - After working on a problem, you may realize that there is something else underlying it that is more important. Accept this new problem and start again.

Top Tip

Bounce ideas off people. When you think you have a good idea or a potential answer, do a 'reality check' by asking someone what they think.

Tried and Trusted Techniques

Brainstorming

Brainstorming is a great way to generate lots of ideas in a short amount of time. Its success rests on everyone getting involved and letting their imagination flow. People can be as creative as they want, as all judgement is suspended until the end when the group tries to structure the ideas generated into a set of options.

Steps

1. Gather a group of 5–10 people in a room.
2. Explain what you are there to discuss and give a brief background.
3. Go around the room and get people to give their ideas.
    - Don't be systematic about people speaking, but do get everyone to join in.
    - Make sure everyone understands each point that has been made.
4. Get a scribe to note all the points on a flip chart.
    - Hang the sheets up on the walls for everyone to see.
5. Work through the notes when the group has finished coming up with ideas.
    - Combine similar ideas and discard ones that are irrelevant.

Tips

Top Tip

- Let the ideas flow naturally.

Know what you want to achieve

- Set your goal at the beginning (decide how many ideas you want).

Don't do it in a vacuum

- It works best if people know what they will discuss and have access to some background information prior to the session. If possible, create a fact pack and distribute it 2 days before the session.

Encourage creativity and suspend judgement

- Start with a clean slate.
- Invite lots of suggestions.
- Get everyone to participate.

Put the session's objective before your personal feelings

· Be prepared to have your ideas culled at the end.
· Seek to combine and improve ideas.

Don't let time ruin a good session

· Give yourself enough time but set a time limit of 1–2 hours.
· Give a 5-minute warning before the end of the session.
· Stop at the designated time, unless there is a natural end beforehand.

De Bono's Six Hats

De Bono's Hats is a great way to get people to think differently about the same issue. Each of the six hats represents a different attitude or way of thinking. This is a particularly useful method when you are evaluating the pros and cons of each option. The order in which you wear these hats is entirely up to you and the group. However, it can be helpful to use the hats in a particular sequence.

When Wearing:

1. *The White Hat:* **Look at the facts.**
   · Look only at facts and figures. Think about the information you have and the information you need to make a sound decision.
2. *The Red Hat:* **Consider how you feel.**
   · Don't worry about the facts; think about how you feel about each option. What is your gut reaction to each?
3. *The Green Hat:* **Be creative in your thinking.**
   · Think laterally and creatively about each option. Don't be rigid about what's out there already; open your mind to new ideas.
4. *The Blue Hat:* **Look at the big picture.**
   · Stand back and consider each option in the light of the overall situation. Think about what further thinking and work is required on each option.
5. *The Black Hat:* **Outline what is negative.**
   · Think through what the downsides of each option are. What, in your opinion, won't work.
6. *The Yellow Hat:* **Outline what is positive.**
   · Think through what the benefits of each option are.

The Six Hats method was designed by Edward de Bono and is now widely in use. To make full use of this powerful method proper training is advised (contact The Holst Group, e-mail: holstgp@msn.com). The method is mentioned here with permission and may not be reproduced without permission.

Top Tip

Actually having physical hats at the meeting may help the group get involved.

Top Tip

Try to avoid over-using the Black Hat.

Top Tip

Most people have a natural tendency to wear one of the hats, so try to encourage everyone to wear all six hats for each item discussed.

Dealing with Difficult People

by Diane Berenbaum

Courtesy of Shutterstock.

Six Strategies for Dealing with Difficult People

By Diane Berenbaum

A recent comment from one of my friends caught me off guard, but got me thinking. She said, with a rather accusatory tone, "I bet you actually like the people you work with. Everyone in my company is so difficult!" After chuckling a bit and regaining my composure, I had to admit it: I do like the people in my company—every single one of them. I knew that I was lucky to work in a place where people really care about the work and each other, but this was a great reminder of that incredible fact.

But, isn't everyone difficult at one time or another? Is it really possible to work in a difficult-free zone? What makes someone difficult anyway?

Ask your associates to describe a difficult person and I'm sure they won't hesitate to share a few choice examples. I bet they'll even fall into one of these classifications:

> **Arrogant types:** Profess to know it all and want no help from anyone else, since others are clearly less qualified and worthy.
>
> **Whining types:** Always see the negative side of things and are constantly complaining about it.
>
> **Demanding types:** Want things done faster, neater, and more thorough than humanly possible and will issue threats if their demands are not met.
>
> **Uncooperative types:** Fail to meet commitments and will ignore multiple requests, deadlines, or even threats for their participation.
>
> **Inconsistent types:** Say one thing, do another and often claim they never committed to doing the first thing in the first place.
>
> **Lackadaisical types:** Don't seem to care about anything and don't take much care with the quality of their work.

Any of these sound familiar? The fact is—anyone who doesn't behave as we expect can be considered difficult and make our lives difficult in the process.

Reacting to Difficult People

Let's face it; difficult people have a way of bringing us down. A friend recently described a conversation he had with an arrogant type and exclaimed, "I just want to smack her!" Yes, this is a common reaction (though, fortunately, it is rarely carried out).

Another associate complained about an uncooperative co-worker who rarely followed through on his commitments and almost always missed deadlines. Her response—total frustration ("He drives me crazy!") and a lack of trust that he will ever come through when she needs him. Chances are she'll pad the deadlines she gives him or just go elsewhere the next time she needs help.

With whiners, we may want to tell them to stop the insanity and quit their bellyaching. After a while, we just stop listening to anything they say (even when they are whining about a legitimate concern).

We may feel pushed or threatened when dealing with a demanding person—and decide that leaving the department or the company would be better than facing those unreasonable demands every day.

And, we tend to lose respect for, and ultimately even ignore, those who are inconsistent or lackadaisical.

These responses, while perfectly natural and understandable, don't tend to yield the best results. Often, we miss important information or get so distracted that we lose sight of the task at hand.

In fact, we might become so annoyed and irritable that it affects our own behavior, so much so that we are perceived as difficult by someone else. And, if we are the difficult person in question, well, you know how others are going to be thinking about and treating us.

Make a Change with Six Thoughtful Strategies

While we cannot avoid crossing paths with difficult people—in our jobs, friendships, and yes, sometimes even our families—we can do something about it. It takes work, but it is definitely worth the effort.

Here are six ways to approach dealing with difficult people:

1. **Avoid Labeling or Judging People**

   If you think you are dealing with a difficult person, you are setting up the conversation to be difficult. Subconsciously, you may put people in categories and then expect them to behave that same way every time.

   For example, your inner-talk about co-worker Jack may go something like this, "Oh that Jack is such a crab; he's going to complain about anything I suggest. I hate talking with him."

   These thoughts that occur before the conversation even takes place may actually negatively impact the nature and outcome of the conversation. Resist the temptation to label or judge, even if their behavior is irritating or disturbing.

2. **Step Back Before You Respond**

   Your natural response to a difficult person may be a quick or critical comeback. Stop yourself! That response may, in fact, come back to haunt you and cause the conversation to go spiraling downward.

   Trust that the other person does not mean to be difficult. The more you can separate the behavior from the person, the less likely you'll be to interpret their behavior as a personal attack. Take time to compose yourself and think of your response, instead of reacting immediately.

3. **Stop Wishing They Were Different**

   How many times have you thought, "If only she would be more responsive, positive, or reliable?"

   Stop wasting your precious mental energy on a futile effort as you've probably realized by now that wishing doesn't work. Difficult people are not irritating you on purpose—and the best way to see a change in them is to change your own thinking and behavior.

4.   **Use a Learning Mindset Approach**

Approach each interaction with an open mind—avoid making decisions or predictions before you start. Really listen to what the other person has to say and remain open to their viewpoint. When people feel your support, they will be more willing to work with you.

Practice using this approach with a friend and see if he or she notices a difference. Or, seek help and feedback from someone you trust. A little candid feedback can get you back on track after a slip into auto-pilot mode.

5.   **Acknowledge vs. Argue**

Our first reaction may be to argue and defend our case. When someone makes an unrealistic demand, we might blast out with a snappy retort like, "That can't be done!" or "That's not realistic," which can only lead the conversation spiraling downward (see point two above).

Instead, acknowledge their perspective and offer to collaborate on next steps. For example, "I can see that this is urgent and you want the system fixed by tomorrow morning. It is more complex than it may seem. I would like to take a moment to go over it and explore a time-frame that will ensure that it is fixed properly and completely." This type of response will not only position you as more of a partner, it will also lead to a better conclusion for both parties.

6.   **Don't Be a Difficult Person Yourself!**

It is easy to identify someone else being difficult. But, how many times do you look in the mirror and acknowledge that you are the one being difficult, especially when you are pushed, cajoled, or just plain tired?

Know thyself and recognize what triggers your own responses. Take responsibility for your actions without turning to your "dark side" so you don't become the difficult person that others avoid.

By changing your attitude and approach towards difficult people, you'll gain a wealth of knowledge, build relationships, and feel a whole lot better. You'll also find that others respond differently to you because they sense your support and willingness to listen.

And maybe someday, when a friend tells you about his difficult co-workers, you too can smile and say that your workplace is not really very difficult at all.

http://www.communicoltd.com/pages/465_six_strategies_for_dealing_with_difficult_people.cfm

Summary of Leadership Theories/Approaches

Theory & Dates	Based On	Major Assumptions	Major Criticisms
Great Man (mid 1800s–early 1900s)	Based on Kings and being born into leadership—ignored great women like Joan of Arc; Catherine the Great	· Leadership development is based on Darwinistic principles (heredity) · Leaders are born, not made · Leaders have natural abilities of power & influence	· Scientific research has not proven that leadership is based on hereditary factors · Leadership was believed to exist only in a few individuals
Trait (1904–1947)	Leaders have a specific set of traits and/or characteristics such as intelligence, height, self-confidence	· A leader has superior or endowed qualities · Certain individuals possess a natural ability to lead · Leaders have traits that differentiate them from followers	· Does not consider the situation · Many traits are too obscure to measure & observe · Research has not adequately linked traits with leadership effectiveness · Most trait studies omit leadership behaviors & followers' motivation and mediating variables
Behavioral (1950s–early 1980s)	Known as "THE ONE BEST WAY TO LEAD" approach	· There is one best way to lead · Leaders who show high concern for both people & production (or consideration & structure) will be effective	· Situation variables & differences in group processes are ignored · Research failed to identify the situations where specific types of leadership behaviors are relevant
Situational Contingency (1950s–1960s)	Vary the leadership approach based on context or situation	· Leaders act differently, depending on the situation · The situation determines who will emerge as the leader · Different leadership behaviors are required for different situations	· Most situational theories are ambiguous & hard to formulate specific, testable propositions · Theories lack accurate measures

Theory & Dates	Based On	Major Assumptions	Major Criticisms
Influence (mid 1920s–1977)	Leadership is based on charisma	· Leadership is an influence process	· More research is needed on the effect charisma has on the leader-follower interaction
Reciprocal/Relational (1978–present)	Mutual goals of leaders and followers are important	· Leadership is a relational process between the leader and the followers · Leadership is a shared process between the leader and the followers · Emphasis is on followership	· Research is lacking · Further clarification is needed on similarities & differences between charismatic & transforming leadership · Processes of collaboration, change, & empowerment are difficult to achieve & measure
Chaos or Systems (1990 to present)	Control is not possible because the world is complex & rapidly changing, so leadership is viewed as an influence relationship and systems are emphasized	· Attempts to describe leadership within a context, where the world is complex & rapidly changing · Leadership is a relational process · Control is impossible, so leadership is described as an influence relationship · Systems are important & emphasized	· Research is lacking · Concepts are difficult to define & understand · The holistic approach makes it hard to achieve and measure

Summary of Leadership Theories/Approaches. Adapted from Komives, S.R., Lucas, N., and McMahon, T.R. (2007) *Exploring Leadership: For college students who want to make a difference* (2nd ed.). San Francisco: Jossey-Bass.

Glossary

abusive boss: a boss who is constantly belittling or intimidating his or her employees

accommodating conflict management style: a conflict management style that allows the other party to have his or her own way without knowing there was a conflict

accountability: accepting the responsibility to perform and reporting back to whoever gave the power

active listening: when a receiver provides a sender full attention without distraction

adjourning stage: when team members bring closure to a project

aggressive behavior: the behavior of an individual who stands up for his or her rights in a manner that violates others' rights in an offensive manner

appearance: how you look

assertive behavior: the behavior of an individual who stands up for his or her rights without violating the rights of others

assets: items that you own that are worth money

attitude: a strong belief toward people, things, and situations

autocratic leaders: leaders who make decisions on their own without input from others

automatic deduction plan: when funds are automatically deducted from an employee's paycheck and placed into a bank account

avoiding conflict management style: a passive conflict management style used when one does not want to deal with the conflict so the offense is ignored

behavioral interview question: interview question that asks candidates to share a past experience related to a specific workplace situation

board of directors: a group of individuals responsible for developing the company's overall strategy and major policies

brainstorming: a problem-solving method that involves identifying alternatives that allow members to freely add ideas while other members withhold comments on the alternatives

budget: a detailed financial plan used to allocate money for a specific time period

business letter: a formal written form of communication used when a message is being sent to an individual outside of an organization

business memo: written communication sent within an organization (also called *interoffice memorandum*)

capital budget: a financial plan used for long-term investments including land and large pieces of equipment

career objective: an introductory written statement used on a résumé for individuals with little or no work experience

casual workdays: workdays when companies relax the dress code policy

chain of command: identifies who reports to whom within the company

character: the unique qualities of an individual, which usually reflect personal morals and values

charismatic power: a type of personal power that makes people attracted to you

chronological résumé layout: a résumé layout used by those with extensive career experience that emphasizes related work experience, skills, and significant accomplishments

coercive power: power that uses threats and punishment

collaborating conflict management style: a conflict management style in which both parties work together to arrive at a solution without having to give up something of value

communication: the process of a sender transmitting a message to an individual (receiver) with the purpose of creating mutual understanding

company resources: financial (fiscal), human (employees), and capital (long-term investments) resources that the company can utilize to achieve its goals

competent: having the ability to answer questions when a customer asks

compromising conflict management style: a conflict management style that is used when both parties give up something of importance to arrive at a mutually agreeable solution to the conflict

confidential: matters that should be kept private

conflict: a disagreement or tension between two or more parties (individuals or groups)

conflict of interest: when someone influences a decision that directly or indirectly benefits him or her

connection power: based on using someone else's legitimate power

continual learning: the ongoing process of increasing knowledge in the area of your career

corporate culture (organizational culture): values, expectations, and behavior of people at work; the company's personality being reflected through employees' behavior

cost of living: average cost of basic necessities such as housing, food, and clothing for a specific geographic area

courtesy: exercising manners, respect, and consideration toward others

cover letter: a letter that introduces your résumé

creativity: the ability to produce something new and unique

credit report: a detailed credit history on an individual

culture: different behavior patterns of various groups

customer service: the treatment an employee provides the customer

debt: money owed

decoding: when a receiver interprets a message

delegate: when a manager or leader assigns part or all of a project to someone else

democratic leaders: leaders who make decisions based upon input from others

demotion: when an employee is moved to a lower position with less responsibility and a decrease in pay

dental benefits: insurance coverage for teeth

department: sub-area of a division that carries out specific functions respective of its division

dependable: being reliable and taking responsibility to assist a customer

development: sessions to enhance or increase existing skills

direct benefits: monetary employee benefits

directional statements: a company's mission, vision, and values statements; these statements are the foundation of a strategic plan explaining why a company exists and how it will operate

diversity statements: corporate statements that remind employees that diversity in the workplace is an asset and not a form of prejudice and stereotyping

diversity training: company training designed to teach employees how to eliminate workplace discrimination and harassment

division: how companies arrange major business functions

documentation: a formal record of events or activities

dress code: an organization's policy regarding appropriate workplace attire

e-dentity: another name for an electronic image

electronic formatted résumés: résumés that are submitted in American Standard Code for Information Interchange (ASCII) format

electronic image: the image formed when someone is communicating and/or researching you through electronic means such as personal web pages and search engines

electronic job search portfolio: a computerized folder that contains electronic copies of all documents kept in hard-copy job search portfolio

employee assistance program (EAP): an employee benefit that typically provides free and confidential psychological, financial, and legal advice

employee handbook: a formal document provided by the company that outlines an employee's agreement with the employer regarding work conditions, policies, and benefits

employee loyalty: an employee's obligation to consistently support a company and its mission

employee morale: the attitude employees have toward the company

employee orientation: a time when a company provides new employees important information including the company's purpose, structure, major policies, procedures, benefits, and other matters

employment-at-will: a legal term for noncontract employees that states that an employee can quit any time he or she wishes

empowerment: pushing power and decision making to the individuals who are closest to the customer in an effort to increase quality, customer satisfaction, and, ultimately, profits

encoding: identifying how a message will be sent (verbally, written, or nonverbally)

entrepreneur: someone who assumes the risk of succeeding or failing in business through owning and operating the business

ethics: a moral standard of right and wrong

ethics statement: a formal corporate policy that addresses the issue of ethical behavior and punishment should someone behave inappropriately

ethnocentric: when an individual believes his or her culture is superior to others

etiquette: a standard of social behavior

executive presence: having the attitude of an executive

executives (senior managers): typically have title of vice president; individuals who work with the president of a company in identifying and implementing the company strategy

exit interview: when an employer meets with an employee who is voluntarily leaving a company to identify opportunities to improve the work environment

expense: money going out

expert power: power that is earned by one's knowledge, experience, or expertise

external customers: customers outside of the company including vendors and the individuals or businesses that purchase a company's product

extrinsic rewards: rewards that come from external sources including such things as money and praise

Fair Isaac Corporation (FICO) score: the most common credit rating

feedback: when a receiver responds to a sender's message based upon the receiver's interpretation of the original message

finance and accounting department: a department that is responsible for the securing, distribution, and growth of the company's financial assets

firing: when an employee is terminated because of a performance issue

fixed expenses: expenses that do not change from month to month

flexible expenses: expenses that change from month to month

forcing conflict management style: a conflict management style that deals with the issues directly

formal communication: workplace communication that occurs through lines of authority

formal learning: returning to college to increase knowledge or improve skills or receive an additional or advanced degree

formal teams: developed within the formal organizational structure and may include functional teams or cross-functional teams

forming stage: when team members first get to know each other and form initial opinions about other members

full-time employee: an employment status for employees who work forty or more hours per week

functional résumé layout: a résumé layout that emphasizes relevant skills when related work experience is lacking

furloughs: when employees are required to take unpaid work days

glass ceiling: invisible barrier that frequently makes executive positions off-limits to females and minorities, thus prohibiting them from advancing up the corporate ladder through promotions

glass wall: invisible barrier that frequently makes certain work areas such as a golf course off-limits to females and minorities, thus prohibiting them from advancing up the corporate ladder through promotions

goal: a target

good: a tangible item produced by a company

good boss: a boss who is respectful and fair

gossip: personal information about another individual that is hurtful and inappropriate

grapevine: an informal communication network where employees talk about workplace issues of importance

grievance: a problem or conflict that occurs in a union setting

grievance procedure: formal steps taken in resolving a conflict between the union and an employer

gross income: the amount of money in a paycheck before paying taxes or other deductions

group interview: an interview that involves several applicants interviewing with each other while being observed by company representatives

harassment: offensive, humiliating, or intimidating behavior

hostile behavior harassment: any behavior of a sexual nature by another employee that someone finds offensive, including verbal slurs, physical contact, offensive photos, jokes, or any other offensive behavior of a sexual nature

human relations: interactions occurring with and through people

human resource department (HR): a department responsible for hiring, training, compensation, benefits, performance evaluations, complaints, promotions, and changes in work status

implied confidentiality: an obligation to not share information with individuals with whom the business is of no concern

income: money coming in

indirect benefits: nonmonetary employee benefits such as health care and paid vacations

informal communication: workplace communication that occurs among individuals without regard to the formal lines of authority

informal learning: increasing knowledge by reading career-related magazines, newsletters, and other articles associated with a job

informal team: group of individuals who get together outside of the formal organizational structure to accomplish a goal

information heading: a résumé heading that contains relevant contact information including name, mailing address, city, state, ZIP code, contact phone, and e-mail address

information power: power based upon an individual's ability to obtain and share information

information systems (IS) department: a business function that deals with the electronic management of computer-based information within the organization

informational interview: when a job seeker meets with a business professional to learn about a specific career, company, or industry

innovation: the process of turning a creative idea into reality

interest: the cost of borrowing money

internal customers: fellow employees and departments that exist within a company

interview portfolio: a folder to be taken on an interview that contains photocopies of documents and items relevant to a position

intrinsic rewards: internal rewards that include such things as self-satisfaction and pride of accomplishment

introductory employee: newly hired full-time employee who has not yet successfully passed his or her introductory period

involuntary termination: when an employee loses his or her job against his or her will

job burnout: a form of extreme stress where you lack motivation and no longer have the desire to work

job description: a document that outlines specific job duties and responsibilities for a specific position

job search portfolio: a collection of paperwork needed for job searches and interviews

job-specific skills: skills that are directly related to a specific job or industry

labeling: when one describes an individual or group of individuals based upon past actions

laissez-faire leaders: leaders who allow team members to make their own decisions without input from the leader (also known as *free reign leaders*)

lateral move: when an employee is transferred to another area (department) of an organization with the same level of responsibility

layoff: when a company releases employees as a result of a company's inability to keep the position

leadership: a process of one person guiding one or more individuals toward a specific goal

learning style: the method of how you best take in information and/or learn new ideas

legal counsel: a function within a business that handles all legal matters relating to the company

legitimate power: the power that is given to an employee from the company

letter of recommendation: a written testimony from another person that states that a job candidate is credible

letter of resignation: a written notice of your voluntary termination

letterhead: paper that has the company logo, mailing address, and telephone numbers imprinted on quality paper

levels of ethical decisions: the first level is the law; the second level is fairness; the third level is one's conscience

liability: an obligation to pay what you owe

life plan: a written document that identifies goals in all areas of your life

listening: the act of hearing attentively

loan: a large debt that is paid in smaller amounts over a period of time and has interest added to the payment

locus of control: identifies who you believe controls your future

long-term goal: a target that takes longer than one year to accomplish

marketing: responsible for creating, pricing, selling, distributing, and promoting the company's product

McClelland's Theory of Needs: holds that people are primarily motivated by one of three factors: achievement, power, or affiliation

mediator: a neutral third party whose objective is to assist two conflicting parties in coming to a mutually agreeable solution

medical benefits: insurance coverage for physician and hospital visits

meeting agenda: an outline of all topics and activities that are to be addressed during a meeting

meeting chair: the individual who is in charge of a meeting and has prepared the agenda

mentor: someone who can help an employee learn more about his or her present position, provide support, and help develop the employee's career

middle manager: typically has the title of *director* or *manager;* these individuals work on tactical issues

mirror words: words that describe the foundation of how you view yourself, how you view others, and how you will most likely perform in the workplace

mission statement: a company's statement of purpose

money wasters: small expenditures that consume a larger portion of one's income than expected

morals: a personal standard of right and wrong

motivation: an internal drive that causes people to behave a certain way to meet a need

negative stress: an unproductive stress that affects your mental and/or physical health including becoming emotional or illogical or losing your temper

negotiation: working with another party to create a situation (resolution) that is fair to all involved parties

net income: the amount of money you have after all taxes and deductions are paid

net worth: the amount of money that is yours after paying off debt

network list: an easily accessible list of all professional network contacts' names, industries, addresses, and phone numbers

networking: meeting and developing relationships with individuals outside one's immediate work area; the act of creating professional relationships

noise: anything that interrupts or interferes with the communication process

non-listening: when a receiver does not make any effort to hear or understand the sender's message

nonverbal communication: what is communicated through body language

norming stage: when team members accept other members for who they are

objectives: short-term goals that are measurable and have specific time lines that occur within one year

one-on-one interview: an interview that involves a one-on-one meeting between the applicant and a company representative

open-door policy: a management philosophy, the purpose of which is to communicate to employees that management and the human resource department are always available to listen should the employees have a concern or complaint

operational budget: a financial plan used for short-term items including payroll and the day-to-day costs associated with running a business

operational issue: organizational issues that typically occur on a daily basis and/or no longer than one year

operations: a business function that deals with the production and distribution of a company's product

operations manager: first-line manager who is typically called a *supervisor* or *assistant manager*

organizational chart: a graphic visual display of how a company organizes its resources; identifies key functions within the company and shows the formal lines of authority for employees

organizational structure: the way a company is organized

panel interview: an interview that involves the applicant meeting with several company employees at the same time

part-time employee: an employment status for employees who work fewer than forty hours a week

passive behavior: the behavior exhibited when an individual does not stand up for his or her rights by consistently allowing others to have their way

passive listening: the receiver is selectively hearing parts of a message

perception: one's understanding or interpretation of reality

performance evaluation: a formal appraisal that measures an employee's work performance

performing stage: when team members begin working on their task

personal commercial: a brief career biography that conveys one's career choice, knowledge, skills, strengths, abilities, and experiences

personal financial management: the process of controlling personal income and expenses

personal profile: an introductory written statement used on a résumé for individuals with professional experience related to their target career

personality: a stable set of traits that assist in explaining and predicting an individual's behavior

physiological needs: an individual's need for basic wages to obtain food, shelter, and other basic needs

politics: obtaining and utilizing power

positive self-talk: a mental form of positive self-reinforcement that helps remind you that you are qualified and deserve both the interview and the job

positive stress: productive stress that provides strength to accomplish a task

power: one's ability to influence another's behavior

power words: action verbs that describe your accomplishments in a lively and specific way

prejudice: a favorable or unfavorable judgment or opinion toward an individual or group based on one's perception (or understanding) of a group, individual, or situation

president or chief executive officer (CEO): the individual responsible for operating the company; this individual takes his or her direction from the board of directors

priorities: determine what needs to be done and in what order

procrastination: putting off tasks until a later time

product: what is produced by a company

productivity: to perform a function that adds value to a company

professionalism: workplace behaviors that result in positive business relationships

profit: revenue (money coming in from sales) minus expenses (the costs involved in running the business)

projection: the way you feel about yourself is reflected in how you treat others

promotion: moving to a position higher in the organization with increased pay and responsibility

proxemics: the study of distance (space) between individuals

quality: a predetermined standard that defines how a product is to be produced

quid pro quo harassment: a form of sexual harassing behavior that is construed as reciprocity or payback for a sexual favor

race: a group of individuals with certain physical traits

reciprocity: creating debts and obligations for doing something

respect: holding someone in high regard

responsibility: accepting the power that is being given and the obligation to perform

responsive: being aware of a customer's needs, often before the customer

restructuring: when a company eliminates a position due to a change in corporate strategy

résumé: a formal written profile that presents a person's knowledge, skills, and abilities to potential employers

retirement: when an employee voluntarily leaves the company and will no longer work

retirement plan: a savings plan for retirement purposes

reward power: the ability to influence someone with something of value

right to revise: a statement contained in many employee handbooks that provides an employer the opportunity to change or revise existing policies

Robert's Rules of Order: a guide to running meetings, oftentimes referred to as *parliamentary procedure*

safety needs: an individual's need for a safe working environment and job security

self-actualization: when an employee has successfully had his or her needs met and desires to assist others in meeting their needs

self-concept: how you view yourself

self-discovery: the process of identifying key interests and skills built upon career goals

self-efficacy: your belief in your ability to perform a task

self-esteem needs: an individual's need for public titles, degrees, and awards

self-image: your belief of how others view you

sender: an individual wanting to convey a message

senior managers or executives: individuals who work with the president in identifying and implementing the company strategy

service: an intangible product produced by a company

sexual harassment: unwanted advances of a sexual nature

shop steward: a coworker who assists others with union-related issues and procedures

short-term goals: goals that can be reached within a year's time (also called *objectives*)

slang: an informal language used among a particular group

SMART goal: a goal that is specific, measurable, achievable, relevant, and time-based

social needs: an individual's need for investment in workplace relationships

soft skills: people skills that are necessary when working with others in the workplace

stereotyping: making a generalized image of a particular group or situation

storming stage: when team members have conflict with each other

strategic issues: major company goals that typically range from three to five years or more

strategic plan: a formal document that is developed by senior management; the strategic plan identifies how the company secures, organizes, utilizes, and monitors its resources

strategy: a company's road map for success that outlines major goals and objectives

stress: a body's reaction to tense situations

structured interview question: a type of interview question that addresses job-related issues where each applicant is asked the same question

supervisor: first-level manager who concerns him- or herself with operational issues

synergy: two or more individuals working together and producing more than the sum of their individual efforts

tactical issues: business issues that identify how to link the corporate strategy into the reality of day-to-day operations; the time line for tactical issues is one to three years

targeted job search: job search process of discovering positions for which you are qualified in addition to identifying specific companies for which you would like to work

team: a group of people linked to a common purpose

teleconference: an interactive communication that connects participants through the telephone without the opportunity of visually seeing all participants

temporary employee: an employee who is hired only for a specified period of time, typically to assist with busy work periods or to temporarily replace an employee on leave

time management: how you manage your time

trade-off: giving up one thing to do something else

training: the process of learning new job skills for the purpose of an employee promotion and/or increased responsibility

transferable skills: skills that can be transferred from one job to another

union: a third-party organization that protects the rights of employees and represents employee interests to an employer

union contract: the formal document that addresses specific employment issues including the handling of grievances, holidays, vacations, and other issues

unstructured interview question: a probing, open-ended interview question intended to identify if the candidate can appropriately sell his or her skills

value: getting a good deal for the price paid for a product

values: things that are important to an individual

values statement: part of a company strategic plan that defines what is important to (or what the priorities are for) the company

verbal communication: the process of using words to send a message

video conference: a form of interactive communication using two-way video and audio technology

virtual teams: teams that function through electronic communications because they are geographically dispersed

vision benefits: insurance coverage for vision (eye) care

vision statement: part of a company's strategic plan that describes the company's viable view of the future

voluntary termination: leaving a job on your own

Vroom's Expectancy Theory: holds that individuals will behave in a certain manner based upon the expected outcome

work recall: when employees are called back to work after a layoff

work wardrobe: clothes that are primarily worn only to work and work-related functions

workplace bullies: employees who are intentionally rude and unprofessional to coworkers

workplace discrimination: acting negatively toward someone based on race, age, gender, religion, disability, or other areas

workplace diversity: differences among coworkers including culture, race, age, gender, economic status, and religion

written communication: a form of business communication that is printed, handwritten, or sent electronically

Index